the knot
guide to
wedding vows
& traditions

the knot
guide to
wedding vows
& traditions

Readings, rituals, music, dances, and toasts

carley roney

and the editors of TheKnot.com

CLARKSON POTTER/PUBLISHERS

NEW YORK

Published in the United States by Clarkson Potter/Publishers, an imprint of the
Crown Publishing Group, a division of Random House, Inc., New York.
www.crownpublishing.com
www.clarksonpotter.com

CLARKSON POTTER is a trademark and POTTER with colophon is a registered
trademark of Random House, Inc.

Due to limitations of space, text permissions appear on pages 205–210,
and photo credits appear on page 211.

A previous edition of this work was published in the United States by
Broadway Books, a division of Random House, Inc., New York, in 2000.

Library of Congress Cataloging-in-Publication Data
Roney, Carley.
   The knot guide to wedding vows and traditions : readings, rituals, music, dances, and
toasts / Carley Roney. — Revised ed.
       p. cm.
   1. Marriage customs and rites. 2. Wedding etiquette. I. Title.
   GT2690.R66 2013
   392.5—dc23   2012028894

ISBN 978-0-7704-3379-6
eISBN 978-0-7704-3382-6

Printed in the United States of America

Front cover photographs (clockwise from top left): She-n-He Photography
and Design, Green Apple Photo, Barbara Alessandra Photography, Melissa
Brandman Photography, Cappy Hotchkiss, Millie Holloman Photography,
Katelyn James Photography, Mike Larson

10   9   8   7   6   5   4

First Revised Edition

contents

CHAPTER FOUR
*Programs
and Quotes*

4

CHAPTER FIVE
Music and Dances

5

CHAPTER SIX
*Speeches
and Toasts*

6

ACKNOWLEDGMENTS

The idea for this book came directly from the millions of brides and grooms who visit TheKnot.com—"vows" and "music" are two of the most searched terms on the site! Their ideas and suggestions were invaluable in our researching and writing this book. So thank you all—particularly the couples who let us reproduce their original, and very moving, vows, photographs, and personal stories. (Thanks as well to their photographers for letting us use their photos. See their credits in the back of the book.)

Many experts in the field gave this book depth. I'd particularly like to thank the celebrants who let us print the unique ceremony words that they have written, especially Barbara Ann Michaels, the Reverend Gary Rozman, Chris Robinson, Bill Swetmon, Joyce Gioia, Joan Hawxhurst, the Reverends Irwin and Florence Schnurman, ordained lay clergyman Noah R. W. Saunders, and Dr. Tino Ballesteros. Thanks as well to the DJs and bandleaders—Steve McEwen, Reid Spears, and Ted Knight—who helped us put together the world's longest song list of first-dance songs.

I'd like to thank all the friends and colleagues and family who have shown brilliant insights and support along the way. I am very lucky to have an incredible team at The Knot to help me pull this together. Thanks to all who contributed, from research to reading to finding the images. Thanks to the Clarkson Potter team, including Aliza Fogelson, Rae Ann Spitzenberger, Zach Greenwald, and Alexis Mentor. Of course, thanks to my family: my husband, David; my children, Havana, Cairo, and Dublin; my father, who introduced me to the brilliance of Rilke; and my mother, the poet in the family.

introduction

With all the details of planning a wedding reception, the ceremony is
often the last thing you think about. But it is, of course, where the
ultimate meaning lies—and despite the traditions and age-old rituals,
you still have plenty of opportunities to express yourselves. The
decisions you make for your wedding (even the choice to have one at
all) give you the chance to make a statement—about what you love
about your relationship and about what is important to you both as
you begin your life together. This book will help you to make your
wedding as unique as you are. Here's what to remember as you plan:

dare to be different

Your wedding should be rich with personality and culture. Think about all of the
things that have meaning for you, and feel free to include them even if they are not
wedding-specific (and even if that means having the words to an obscure song on
your invitation). What's most important is that the lyrics, readings, and sayings are
significant to you. The worst thing that can happen is that people will ask questions
and you might have the chance to let them in on the secret. And don't be afraid to
make people laugh!

get swept away

Even if you won't have readings at your wedding, spend a few evenings together
indulging in the words about love and marriage that we've included in this book.
They'll make you think, they'll make you cry, and they'll put into perspective any
tensions the wedding planning may be causing you.

put it in your own words

No, you don't have to literally compose your entire ceremony. Just make sure you choose words that have meaning for you, and that you actually think about that meaning. Also, put away any preconceived notions you may have about religious words—they can be some of the most moving.

If you find additional readings you love or a perfect first-dance song that we have left out, let us know! Come to The Knot and submit your ideas, or find even more at:

TheKnot.com/Ceremony

TheKnot.com/Traditions

TheKnot.com/Vows

TheKnot.com/Rituals

TheKnot.com/Programs

TheKnot.com/Music

TheKnot.com/Toasts

Enjoy!

the knot
guide to
wedding vows
& traditions

YOUR VOWS

Before you ever read a single sample of some traditional or even new vows, take a few minutes to think about what themes you want your vows to incorporate or touch upon. What's important to you? Jot down some ideas here.

1

VOWS

While it's inevitable that most of the planning goes into the party, a wedding is ultimately about making a public promise. To be legally wed, all you really need to do is consent to marry each other before an authorized officiant: "Max, do you take Maria as your lawfully wedded wife?" "I do" (and vice versa) basically does it. But we're not going to let you off the hook that easily. Invest some time thinking through your commitment to each other. Whether you work with your own words or traditional vows, we want you to really mean what you are saying.

TRADITIONAL RELIGIOUS VOWS

Each religious faith has wedding traditions and practices, including marriage vows that have been passed down through generations. The exact phrases used vary slightly from place to place and among different clergy—your officiant will most likely give you an outline that describes the entire ceremony as he or she generally performs it, as well as printed vows, which you may decide to use verbatim or as a jumping-off point. Here you will find the common wordings and a few notes on the ceremony for each religion as well as various denominations. Don't be afraid to respectfully ask your priest, minister, or rabbi for a departure from the words they usually use.

protestant vows

There are many different types of Protestant churches, all with their own slightly different traditions and beliefs. There are also nondenominational Protestant churches that do not affiliate themselves with a larger religious organization. Talk to your chosen officiant about what vows he or she traditionally suggests. Below are guidelines for several denominations; you will find that many of them differ only slightly from one another. Most are based on the Protestant Book of Common Prayer.

BASIC PROTESTANT VOWS

"I, _____ , take thee, _____ , to be my wedded wife/husband, to have and to hold, from this day forward, for better, for worse, for richer, for poorer, in sickness and in health, to love and to cherish, till death do us part, according to God's holy ordinance; and thereto I pledge thee my faith [or] pledge myself to you [or] plight thee my troth."

LUTHERAN VOWS

"I take you, _____ , to be my wife/husband from this day forward, to join with you and share all that is to come, and I promise to be faithful to you until death parts us."

"I, _____ , take you, _____ , to be my wife/husband, and these things I promise you: I will be faithful to you and honest with you; I will respect, trust, help, and care for you; I will share my life with you; I will forgive you as we have been forgiven; and I will try with you better to understand ourselves, the world, and God; through the best and the worst of what is to come, as long as we live."

EPISCOPAL VOWS

"_____ , will you have this woman/man to be your wedded wife/husband to live together in the covenant of marriage? Will you love her/him, comfort her/him, honor and keep her/him, in sickness and in health, and forsaking all others be faithful to her/him as long as you both shall live?"

METHODIST VOWS

"Will you have this woman/man to be your wife/husband, to live together in a holy marriage? Will you love her/him, comfort her/him, honor and keep her/him in sickness and in health, and forsaking all others, be faithful to her/him as long as you both shall live?"

"In the name of God, I, _____ , take you, _____ , to be my wife/husband, to have and to hold from this day forward, for better, for worse, for richer, for poorer, in sickness and in health, to love and to cherish, until we are parted by death. This is my solemn vow."

PRESBYTERIAN VOWS

"_____ , wilt thou have this woman/man to be thy wife/husband, and wilt thou pledge thy faith to her/him, in all love and honor, in all duty and service, in all faith and tenderness, to live with her/him, and cherish her/him, according to the ordinance of God, in the holy bond of marriage?"

"I, _____ , take you, _____ , to be my wedded wife/husband, and I do promise and covenant, before God and these witnesses, to be your loving and faithful husband/wife, in plenty and want, in joy and in sorrow, in sickness and in health, as long as we both shall live."

BAPTIST VOWS

"Will you, _____ , have _____ to be your wife/husband? Will you love her/him, comfort and keep her/him, and forsaking all others remain true to her/him, as long as you both shall live?"

"I, _____ , take thee, _____ , to be my wife/husband, and before God and these witnesses I promise to be a faithful and true husband/wife."

putting your best face forward

Traditionally, couples have faced their officiant or each other when reciting their vows—with their backs to all their family and friends. A new trend is for the officiant to stand with his back to the guests, so that the couple is facing the congregation, making them feel more included in what's going on (and making it easier for guests to hear the vows).

⸺ ෴ ⸺

roman catholic vows

A traditional Catholic wedding ceremony takes place as part of a full Mass, but some couples choose a modified, shorter service. Whether you can do so may depend on the church you marry in and on your officiant.

> "I, _____ , take you, _____ , to be my wife/husband. I promise to be true to you in good times and in bad, in sickness and in health. I will love you and honor you all the days of my life."

> "I, _____ , take you, _____ , for my lawful wife/husband, to have and to hold from this day forward, for better, for worse, for richer, for poorer, in sickness and health, until death do us part."

eastern orthodox vows

Eastern Orthodox wedding ceremonies (this includes Greek, Romanian, and Russian Orthodox) are rich with tradition, but often they do not include spoken vows. The rings are blessed and then exchanged between the couple three times, to represent the Holy Trinity of the Father, the Son, and the Holy Spirit. The couple is also traditionally "crowned" with gold crowns connected to each other by a ribbon to symbolize the marriage connection. They are exchanged over the couple's heads three times to officially seal the union. After the bride and groom are led around the wedding platform three times, they are husband and wife.

However, in some denominations, including the Russian Orthodox Church, vows may be spoken aloud. An example:

> "I, _____ , take you, _____ , as my wedded wife/husband, and I promise you love, honor, and respect; to be faithful to you; and not to forsake you until death do us part. So help me God, one in the Holy Trinity, and all the saints."

the church of jesus christ of latter-day saints vows

In the Church of Jesus Christ of Latter-day Saints (also known as the Mormon Church), there are two options for a wedding ceremony. The first is known as a "sealing ceremony" and is performed in a Mormon temple, so only guests who are members of the church and have participated in temple worship can attend. The exact vows that take place in a sealing ceremony are considered private to the church and aren't discussed outside of a temple setting.

ceremony itinerary

The vows are the center of most wedding ceremonies. Religious and cultural rituals differ, of course, but if you were to outline a standard ceremony based on a Christian service, it would look something like this:

PROCESSIONAL
The couple and wedding party enter the ceremony room or sanctuary, usually with accompanying music. The congregation generally stands for the bride's entrance.

OPENING REMARKS
The officiant announces that everyone is there to celebrate the joining of the two of you in marriage; if it's a religious event, he or she may offer a blessing to the congregation.

THE "GIVING AWAY"
If you will have your parents or friends "support you" in your marriage, or if you opt for the tradition of the bride's father giving her away, that happens now. This is also a time for your officiant and you to acknowledge your friends and family and the importance of their presence.

STATEMENT OF PURPOSE/ DECLARATION OF CONSENT
The officiant asks the two of you whether you are each coming of your own free will to marry each other, and if you are prepared to do so. This is your public announcement—to the congregation gathered—of the vows you're about to take.

EXCHANGE OF VOWS
You promise to love each other as long as you both shall live! These are the words you choose to share with each other before those family and friends.

READINGS AND RITUALS
These, as well as additional musical selections, may be incorporated throughout the service. Talk to your officiant and determine the order together, if possible.

RING EXCHANGE
You give each other your wedding bands. The officiant may bless the rings as you do so.

BLESSING/CLOSING REMARKS FROM THE OFFICIANT

DECLARATION OF MARRIAGE
You are pronounced "husband and wife"! You kiss, gathered friends and family may applaud, and the recessional music begins.

RECESSIONAL
You leave the sanctuary as a married couple.

The second ceremony can be performed anywhere (so any guests you choose can attend) by a church officer—usually a bishop. In this situation, the vows are often in the form of a question:

"_____ , do you take _____ as your lawfully wedded wife/ husband, and do you of your own free will and choice covenant as her/his companion and lawfully wedded wife/husband that you will cleave unto him/her and none else; that you will observe all the laws, covenants, and obligations pertaining to the holy state of matrimony; and that you will love, honor, and cherish her/him as long as you both shall live?"

unitarian vows

The Unitarian Universalist Church generally leaves service structure to individual ministers; your officiant may allow you significant freedom to create your own ceremony and vows. Suggested vows may borrow from traditional Christian versions:

"I, _____ , take you, _____ , to be my wife/husband; to have and to hold from this day forward, for better, for worse, for richer, for poorer, in sickness and in health, to love and cherish always."

"_____ , will you take _____ to be your wife/husband; love, honor, and cherish her/him now and forevermore?"

jewish vows

There is no actual exchange of vows in a traditional Jewish ceremony; the covenant is said to be implicit in the ritual. Ceremony structure varies within the Orthodox, Conservative, Reform, and Reconstructionist synagogues, and also among individual rabbis. The marriage vow is customarily sealed when the groom places a ring on his bride's finger and says:

"Behold, you are consecrated to me with this ring according to the laws of Moses and Israel."

However, today many Jewish couples opt for double-ring ceremonies, so the bride may also recite the traditional ring words, or a modified version. The traditional Seven Blessings, or Sheva B'rachot (see page 50), are also an integral part of Jewish wedding ceremonies; they are often recited by relatives and friends of the couple's choosing. And because many Jewish couples today do want to exchange spoken vows, they are now included in many Reform and Conservative ceremonies.

REFORM

"Do you, _____ , take _____ to be your wife/husband, promising to cherish and protect her/him, whether in good fortune or in adversity, and to seek together with her/him a life hallowed by the faith of Israel?"

CONSERVATIVE

"Do you, _____ , take _____ to be your lawfully wedded wife/husband, to love, to honor, and to cherish?"

Another version of nontraditional vows is a phrase from the biblical Song of Songs:

"*Ani leh-dodee veh-dodee lee*": "I am my beloved's, and my beloved is mine."

muslim vows

Muslim couples do not generally recite vows but rather listen to the words of the imam, or cleric (although any adult male Muslim may officiate), who speaks about the significance of the commitment of

---

so little has changed!

If you haven't yet felt the power of tradition in wedding vows, check out these words from the Middle Ages—little has changed, except for Old English spelling, and, in many cases, the "obey" part:

"Wilte thou haue this woman to be thy wedde wife, to liue together after Goddes ordeinuce in the holy estate of matrimonie? Wilt thou loue her, coumforte her, honor, and kepe her in sicknesse and in health? And forsaking all other kepe thee onely to her, so long as you bothe shall liue?"

The man shall aunswere: I will.

Then shall the priest saye to the woman:

"Wilt thou haue this man to be thy wedde houseband, to liue together after Goddes ordienaunce, in the holy estate of matrimonie? Wilt thou abey him and serue him, loue, honor, and kepe him in sicknesse, and in health? And forsaking all other kepe thee onely to him, so long as you bothe shall liue?"

The woman shall aunswere: I will.

Here are a couple of updated versions that would be perfect for a nondenominational, interfaith, or civil ceremony:

"_____ , do you take _____ to be your wife/husband? Do you promise to love, honor, cherish, and protect her/him, forsaking all others and holding only unto her/him?"

"_____ , do you take _____ to be your wife/husband? Do you promise to love, honor, cherish, and protect her/him, forsaking all others and holding only to her/him forevermore?"

---

marriage and the couple's responsibilities toward each other and Allah. The bride and groom are asked three times if they accept each other in marriage according to the terms of their traditional marriage contract, or Nikah. Then they sign and the marriage is sealed; the gathered congregation may bless them.

The ceremony might be augmented with readings from the Koran, the holy book of Islam. You might also consider a "honey ceremony," acknowledging the sharing of the "sweetness of life" (see page 105).

hindu vows

A traditional Hindu wedding ceremony is elaborate and complex, incorporating fifteen specific rituals. There are no "vows" in the Western sense, but the Seven Steps, or Saptha Padhi, around a flame (honoring the fire god, Agni) spell out the promises the couple makes to each other:

> "Let us take the first step to provide for our household a nourishing and pure diet, avoiding those foods injurious to healthy living.

> "Let us take the second step to develop physical, mental, and spiritual powers.

> "Let us take the third step to increase our wealth by righteous means and proper use.

> "Let us take the fourth step to acquire knowledge, happiness, and harmony by mutual love and trust.

> "Let us take the fifth step so that we are blessed with strong, virtuous, and heroic children.

> "Let us take the sixth step for self-restraint and longevity.

> "Finally, let us take the seventh step and be true companions and remain lifelong partners by this wedlock."

See page 100 for the pronouncement made after the couple has completed all seven steps (which also makes a beautiful reading for any type of wedding).

quaker vows

A Quaker wedding usually takes place during a regularly scheduled Meeting of Friends. The congregation and couple all worship silently until the bride and groom feel the time is right to stand and recite their

not hindu?

Get inspired by Hindu wedding traditions. The Seven Steps ritual is a creative format to build your own ceremony ritual around. Decide on seven "missions" or vows you have as a couple and recite them together, as you perform some act: stepping, placing stones or flowers in a vase, or lighting seven candles.

vows to each other. There is no officiant—the Quaker belief is that only God can create the marriage bond. The words below are traditional, but after saying them, couples often speak quite personally to each other.

"In the presence of God and these our friends I take thee, _____ , to be my husband/wife, promising with Divine assistance to be unto thee a loving and faithful wife/husband so long as we both shall live."

buddhist vows

Weddings in Buddhist countries are considered secular affairs, but the couple usually also gets the blessing from monks at the local temple. For a Western couple with no access to such a temple, there is no formal ceremony structure, but usually the couple erects a shrine with a Buddha image, candles, and flowers. They light the candles, as well as incense, and place the flowers around the Buddha as an offering. You may include readings from the Dhammapada, a holy Buddhist book.

Traditional chants to Buddha include the Vandana, Tisarana, and Pancasila. You may also choose to include the traditional Buddhist homily (see page 51). Blessings from friends and family who are present (as well as the couple bowing to their parents out of respect) are also inherent parts of the Buddhist wedding ceremony. There are no official vows; you may choose to say original words to each other.

INTERFAITH AND NONDENOMINATIONAL VOWS

If the two of you are of different religions, you have several ceremony options. You may choose to marry in just one of your houses of worship (if it is allowed by your faith and officiant; ask them for details). You may decide to work with two officiants, one from each faith; if this is the case, you may say two sets of vows. Or you may choose a nondenominational or civil officiant, who will help you create your own blended vows or allow you to write original vows (see the Writing Your Own Vows section on page 29).

Many interfaith couples decide to express their religions in their ceremony's prayers, blessings, or rituals and reserve the vows as a place to talk secularly about their feelings for each other. With this approach, your possible vows are virtually unlimited.

Or perhaps neither of you is religious, or you have other reasons to want a more secular ceremony. You don't have to forgo a spiritual element to your vows. The vows below, many courtesy of officiants who marry couples of all spiritual and religious backgrounds, are appropriate for interfaith and nondenominational couples alike.

From Reverend Gary Rozman, a nondenominational minister:
"Today, I, give myself to you, _____ , and ask for your tomorrows. I promise to love you, laugh with you, and share your dreams. I will give you my strength and ask for yours in return. I wish to be with you always, and ask you to accept me as your wife/husband, best friend, and love for life."

"_____ , do you take _____ to be your spouse and life partner and promise above all else to live in truth with her/him, to communicate fully and fearlessly, to pledge your love, devotion, faith, and honor as both your lives are joined today?"

"I, _____ , take _____ as my wife/husband. To love, admire, and respect; to embrace our distinctions; to find comfort in our similarities and anticipate our evolving personalities. To care for in sickness and in health; to console in times of sadness and celebrate with in times of elation. To feed and sustain always. To honor what I have felt to be true: that our love is but beginning. To cherish and hold her/him, forsaking all others, so long as we both shall live."

From Barbara Ann Michaels, a multifaith wedding officiant:
"_____ , you are my friend, my love, and my partner. As your wife/husband, I will cherish you as my family in our community. I will respect and defend you. I will be open and honest, listen to you, and support you. I will share your strength and peace, your humor and wisdom—in joy and sadness, comfort and adversity, now and forever."

From the Reverends Irwin and Florence Schnurman, interfaith ministers:
"I promise, _____ , before family and friends, to commit my love to you; to respect your individuality; to be with you through life's changes; and to nurture and strengthen the love between us, as long as we both shall live."

From Joan Hawxhurst's book Interfaith Wedding Ceremonies:
"I love you. And I look forward to being your friend and companion, your wife/husband and love for life. I promise to love you and respect you; to stand by you and be faithful to you; to be open and honest

with you; and to always work toward our mutual growth. I promise this with the help of God, for the good times and the bad times, till death do us part."

"I, _____ , cherish you, _____ ,
For being all that you are,
All that you are not,
And all that you can be.
Know that I am here for you,
And that your pain will be mine,
And your joy mine as well.
All I ask is you—your love, your trust, your caring.
I choose you to be my wife/husband."

"I take you to be my wife/husband, my friend, my love, and my lifelong companion: to share my life with yours. To build our dreams together, while allowing you to grow with your dreams; to support you through times of trouble, and rejoice with you in times of happiness; to treat you with respect, love, and loyalty through all the trials and triumphs of our lives together; and to give you all the love I can give my whole life long. This commitment is made in love, kept in faith, lived in hope, and eternally made new."

From Joyce Gioia, multifaith clergywoman:
"I, _____ , choose you, _____ , to be my wife/husband, my friend, my love, the mother/father of our children. I will be yours in plenty and in want, in sickness and in health, in failure and in triumph. I will cherish you and respect you, comfort you and encourage you, and together we shall live, freed and bound by our love."

"_____ , do you now choose _____ to be your wife/husband, to share your life openly with her/him, to speak truthfully and lovingly to her/him, to accept her/him fully as she/he is and delight in who she/he is becoming, to respect her/his uniqueness, encourage her/his fulfillment, and compassionately support her/him through all the changes of your years together?"

"_____ , will you have this woman/man to be your wife/husband, to live together in marriage? Will you love her/him and give her/him your respect? Will you comfort, honor, and keep her/him in sickness and in health, in joy and in sorrow, so long as love and life shall endure?"

craziest wedding vows ever

Some couples completely break with tradition and say some pretty hilarious things.

"I vow that I will always think you're hotter than Robert Pattinson."

"I promise to accept Twizzlers as a food group."

"I promise to love you and be faithful to you for as long as we can stand each other."

"Through fat and skinny."

LOVED ONES AS OFFICIANTS

How can a friend or family member perform our ceremony?
There are a few large organizations that will ordain people for this
purpose via the Internet. Some of the most common online ministries
are the American Fellowship Church, the Universal Life Church,
Universal Ministries, and Rose Ministries. Once you find one that seems
to suit you, check with your secretary of state's office to ensure it is
reputable. The American Fellowship Church, for example, is
legally registered with the California Secretary of State's office
as a nonprofit religious organization in good standing.

How long does it take to get ordained?
The process varies depending on what organization you go through.
The American Fellowship Church ordains instantly via the Internet
and sends ID cards and minister's licenses immediately afterward.
Check with the organization to find out the specifics.

What does our officiant need to do after becoming ordained?
After the wedding, your officiant must complete the marriage license
(for which you usually need two witnesses to sign, along with the couple
and the minister) and mail it to the state or county clerk's office. Each
state has different laws for how soon after the ceremony the license
must be mailed, so make sure you do your homework.

"I, _____ , take you, _____ , as my husband/wife, to care for you
and trust you, to cherish you and respect you, to forgive you and be
forgiven by you. I will love you in good times and in bad, when we are
together and when we are apart. I promise to be ever faithful, today
and for all our tomorrows."

From Bill Swetmon, ordained nondenominational minister:
"_____ , will you take _____ to be your wife/husband? Do you
commit yourself to her/his happiness and self-fulfillment as a person?
Do you promise to love, honor, and trust her/him in sickness and in
health, in adversity and prosperity, and to be true and loyal to her/
him so long as you both shall live?"

"_____ , I promise to be faithful, supportive, and loyal and to
give you my companionship and love throughout all the changes
of our life. I vow to bring you happiness, and I will treasure you as
my companion. I will celebrate the joys of life with you. I promise
to support your dreams, and walk beside you offering courage and

strength through all endeavors. From this day forward, I will be proud to be your wife/husband and your best friend."

"I choose you, _____ , to be my wife/husband, as my friend and love. On this day I affirm the relationship we have enjoyed, looking to the future and to keep and strengthen it. I will be yours in plenty and in want, in sickness and in health, in failure and in triumph. Together, we will dream and live as one while respecting one another; we will stumble but restore each other, we will share all things. I will cherish, comfort, and encourage you, be open with you, and stay with you as long as I shall live."

"I, _____ , take you, _____ , for my wedded wife/husband from this day forward, to have and to hold as equal partner in my life, to whom I give my deepest love and devotion. I humbly open my heart to you as a sanctuary of warmth and peace, where you may come and find a refuge of love and strength. I will love you enough to risk being hurt, trust you when I don't understand, weep with you in heartache, and celebrate life with you in joy. I will receive you as my equal throughout all of our days."

Other nondenominational options:

"I, _____ , take you, _____ , to be no other than yourself. Loving what I know of you, trusting what I do not yet know, I will respect

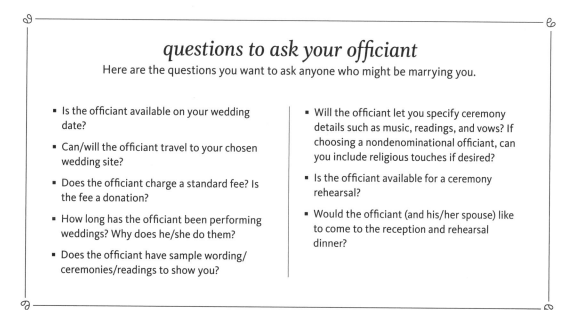

questions to ask your officiant

Here are the questions you want to ask anyone who might be marrying you.

- Is the officiant available on your wedding date?
- Can/will the officiant travel to your chosen wedding site?
- Does the officiant charge a standard fee? Is the fee a donation?
- How long has the officiant been performing weddings? Why does he/she do them?
- Does the officiant have sample wording/ceremonies/readings to show you?

- Will the officiant let you specify ceremony details such as music, readings, and vows? If choosing a nondenominational officiant, can you include religious touches if desired?
- Is the officiant available for a ceremony rehearsal?
- Would the officiant (and his/her spouse) like to come to the reception and rehearsal dinner?

need more ceremony help?

The following books focus on specific types of religious and cultural ceremonies and may further help you to design your ceremony—especially if you are joining multiple religions and/or backgrounds:

- *Jumping the Broom: The African-American Wedding Planner,* 2nd edition, by Harriette Cole (Owl Books, 2004)

- *Vows: The African-American Couples' Guide to Designing a Sacred Ceremony,* by Harriette Cole (Simon & Schuster, 2004)

- *Going to the Chapel: From Traditional to African-Inspired, and Everything in Between—The Ultimate Wedding Guide to Today's Black Couple,* by the editors of *Signature Bride* (Putnam, 1999)

- *African-American Wedding Readings,* edited by Tamara Nikuradse (Plume, 1998)

- *Good Luck Life: The Essential Guide to Chinese American Celebration and Culture,* by Rosemary Gong (William Morrow Paperbacks, 2005)

- *The Complete Book of Christian Wedding Vows: The Importance of How You Say "I Do,"* by H. Norman Wright (Bethany House, 2003)

- *The Catholic Wedding Book: A Complete Guidebook,* by Molly K. Hans and William C. Graham (Paulist Press, 2007)

- *The Protestant Wedding Sourcebook: A Complete Guide for Developing Your Own Service,* by Sidney F. Batts (Westminster John Knox Press, 1993)

- *Gay and Lesbian Weddings: Planning the Perfect Same-Sex Ceremony,* by David Toussaint and Heather Leo (Ballantine Books, 2004)

- *Gay Wedding Confidential,* by Bernadette Coveney Smith (iUniverse, 2010)

- *The Hindu Wedding Planner,* by Angirasa Muni (Sacred Books, 1999)

- *A Comprehensive Indian Wedding Planner,* by Sarbjit K. Gill (Bookmark Press, 2002)

- *Irish Wedding Traditions: Using Your Irish Heritage to Create the Perfect Wedding,* by Shannon McMahon Lichte (Diane Publishing, 2003)

- *Joining Hands and Hearts: Interfaith, Intercultural Wedding Celebrations—A Practical Guide for Couples,* by Susanna Stefanachi Macomb (Atria Books, 2002)

- *Your Interfaith Wedding: A Guide to Blending Faiths, Cultures, and Personal Values into One Beautiful Wedding Ceremony,* by Laurie Sue Brockway (Praeger, 2010)

- *The Creative Jewish Wedding Book: A Hands-on Guide to New and Old Traditions, Ceremonies, and Celebrations,* 2nd edition, by Gabrielle Kaplan-Mayer (Jewish Lights Publishing, 2009)

- *The Everything Jewish Wedding Book: Mazel Tov! From the Chuppah to the Hora, All You Need for Your Big Day,* by Rabbi Hyim Shafner (Adams Media, 2009)

your integrity and have faith in your abiding love for me, through all our years, and in all that life may bring us."

"_____ , I take you as my wife/husband, with your faults and your strengths, as I offer myself to you with my faults and my strengths. I will help you when you need help, and turn to you when I need help. I choose you as the person with whom I will spend my life."

ETHICAL HUMANIST VOWS

Members of Ethical Humanist societies are usually nontheistic—they believe in human ethics without the need of a religious authority. A humanist ceremony in its basic form focuses on the couple's relationship and the fact that they are making a public declaration of their commitment to be married. However, ministers are open to couples creating original ceremonies, even those including spiritual rituals—the officiant simply will not mention God or recite any religious blessings. Here are some basic Ethical Humanist vows.

"_____ , will you receive _____ as your lawfully wedded wife/husband? Will you share your life with her/him, hold your love firm, and dutifully care for her/him in all the varying circumstances of your life?"

"_____ , will you have _____ as your wife/husband, to live together in marriage? Will you love her/him, comfort her/him, and honor her/him, in sickness and in health, in sorrow and in joy, as long as you both shall live?"

"I, _____ , choose you, _____ , to be my wife/husband. I will respect you, care for you, and grow with you, through good times and hard times, as your friend, companion, and partner, giving the best that I can, to fulfill our lives together."

CIVIL VOWS

If you choose to marry in a civil service—at city hall, in a Vegas chapel, or simply with a judge or other public official as your officiant—you will probably use very simple, basic vows. If you plan somewhat in advance, however, your officiant will probably allow you to write your own vows

that's all she quote

Got writer's block? Famous love quotes are a great leaping-off point when creating your own vows—and feel free to use them directly in your vows as a way to add a little more depth to them. Check out Chapter Four (page 113) for our list of lovely quotes.

i take you—who?

Exactly what do you say when you say your partner's name? Your officiant might have couples say the full name of their spouse-to-be ("Robert William Darnell"), or you may just use first names, or perhaps first and middle names. If you aren't having a superformal ceremony, use the name everyone is familiar with—for example, if everyone calls the groom Rex even though his real name is Richard. Unless the celebrant has a policy, this decision will probably be left to you. You actually just need to say the other person's name to make it clear whom you intend to marry!

or recite words of your own choosing. Here are some basic civil vows to start with:

"_____ , do you take _____ as your lawfully wedded wife/husband?"

"_____ , do you take _____ to be your legal wedded wife/husband, to have and to hold from this day forward?"

"_____ , I take you to be my lawfully wedded wife/husband. Before these witnesses I vow to love you and care for you for as long as we both shall live."

SAME-SEX WEDDING VOWS AND COMMITMENT CEREMONIES

The vows of gay and lesbian weddings don't necessarily differ from straight weddings at all. You can use any of the vows you see here or the vows from your house of worship, or you can use these as a starting point, editing them to suit your relationship. Or you can also start from scratch and create a new set of vows all your own. Read on for more tips on writing your own vows. But you will need to consider how to tweak the pronouns and titles (you can be wife and wife, husband and husband, "partners for life," or whatever you choose). Here are two examples of how two same-sex couples chose to be pronounced:

"Anne and Gabrielle, your lives and spirits are joined in a union of love and trust. Your love should be a constant source of light, and like the earth, a firm foundation from which to grow. As you have consented in this ceremony in the presence of friends and family to be partners for life, I now pronounce you spiritually united and bound together body and soul. You may kiss each other."

"Rachel and Jennifer, you have made this solemn covenant of marriage before God and before this gathered community. By the power vested in me by the state, but most of all by the power of your own love, I declare that you are bound to one another in a holy covenant. May God empower you with love and faithfulness all your days."

make a vow date

Go out to dinner or set aside an evening at home to take some time to talk about the important days, events, and turning points in your relationship. Be sure to have notepads and pens handy and to discuss the following:

- When did you fall in love? Why?

- When did you each say "I love you" for the first time?

- What qualities do you most admire in each other?

- What does your partner bring out in you?

- What ways are you alike? Different? How do you complement each other?

- Why did you decide to get married?

- What hard times have you gone through together? What have you supported each other through?

- Did you ever break up or almost break up? What got you back together or made you stay together?

- What do you have together that you don't have apart?

- What challenges do you envision in your future? What do you want to accomplish together?

- What, in your view, is the most important part of marriage?

You may or may not be able to incorporate some of this into your vows—but either way, you will have one romantic date!

WRITING YOUR OWN VOWS

There's something very meaningful about repeating the vows of thousands of brides and grooms before you. But if you aren't constrained for religious reasons to stick with standard vows, we strongly suggest you take a crack at crafting your own. Putting your promises on paper is an emotional, eye-opening, and often extremely memorable experience. Even if you end up with very traditional-sounding words, it will be worth the trip—we promise.

guidelines

We can't say this enough: Start early! Don't leave writing your vows until the day before. You'll be much too nervous, excited, and rattled to give them the time and thought they deserve. Give yourselves at least a month or two, or work on your vows in that pocket of time after you've set up all your major wedding vendors and before you have to start thinking about details. Writing your vows should be done in a relaxed, not rushed, frame of mind. Here are some tips on the process:

- Before you begin, talk about what marriage means to each of you. Discuss what you expect from each other and the relationship; how you each define words like *respect, cherish, love, support, commit,* and *promise,* and how you would prioritize those things; and how you envision yourselves growing older together. Not only will this help you to focus on what kind of vows you want to write—it's good for you! Use your smartphone to record video of your own mini interviews with each other on these topics for inspiration later.

- Examine traditional religious vows—your own, if you practice a certain faith, but others as well—to see what strikes a chord with you. You can incorporate them into the original words you write, or at least use them as a jumping-off point.

- Borrow freely from poetry, love stories, and religious and spiritual texts—even from romantic movies. Jot down words and phrases that capture your feelings. Widely recognized works ring true for a reason. See Chapter Two, Readings (page 41), for inspiration. But don't just think about browsing through poetry books—search Twitter, Tumblr, Pinterest, Google+, and YouTube using hashtags such as #weddingvows.

- Decide whether you will each write your vows separately. If you do, you'll probably run them by each other before the wedding, though saving the words until the wedding day can make for quite an emotional moment. If you want the vows to be a surprise on your wedding day, make sure you each send a copy of what you've written to your officiant or a friend so that she can check that they're about the same length. Some couples write a mutual vow that they will both take, as you would with traditional vows. You may want to test out how it sounds when you read it. Record it on your phone and watch the time.

- Once you've done all your research—talking to each other and looking at traditional vows and other written words of love—start writing! Try to get a first draft together at least two to three weeks before the wedding.

- Your vows can be clever and light, but they should acknowledge the seriousness of the commitment you're about to make. If it's okay with your officiant, it's fine to throw in a humorous comment—"I promise to love you, adore you, and let you watch Monday night football"— but don't make the whole thing a joke. Even if you can take it, your audience might be weirded out.

- Don't make your vows so personal that they're cryptic—or embarrassing! You've invited your family and friends to witness your vows in order to make your bond public, so be sure everyone feels included in the moment.

- Don't make your vows too long. While they are the most important element of your ceremony, that doesn't mean they should go on for hours. Stick to three to five minutes and save some thoughts for toasting at the reception—and for the wedding night. Your vows should get at the heart of what marrying this person means to you; pick the most important points and make them well.

- Ask your officiant if he or she will want to approve your vows before the big day. If you're having a religious ceremony, the officiant most definitely will. She or he may raise faith-based questions—or even objections to some of your wording—but may also contribute interesting thoughts or quotes for you to consider.

- Have a final version at least two days before your wedding. Practice out loud. These are words meant to be heard by an audience, so be sure they sound good when spoken. Avoid tongue twisters and watch out for superlong sentences; you don't want to get out of breath.

- If you plan to read your vows from a tablet or smartphone, make sure there's service where you'll be or use an offline notebook.

- Decide whether you'll memorize your words. Most officiants give this idea the thumbs-down—you'll probably be so nervous or emotional that your mind will go blank! Either read them to each other or have the officiant say them for you to repeat.

- Make sure your guests will be able to hear you! Consider microphones (tiny lavalieres) if your wedding is large or will be held outside. If your guests can't understand, they'll disconnect. You may want to print your vows in your program, so that even if those gathered can't hear every word, they can still follow along.

- Think about whether you want to Livestream your vows. It's a great option if you are having a destination wedding and not everyone can make it. After the ceremony, you can always clip and save any portion and share it. And don't forget to post your photos to Instagram!

renewing your vows

Keep a copy of your vows in a safe place, such as the back of your wedding album. Couples we know have a ritual of reciting their vows again on every anniversary. Others have even renewed their vows in a wedding-like party after five or ten years.

real couples' vows

Below are vows some couples used in their recent weddings. Let them inspire you in writing yours. (We've printed one partner's words to the other; unless otherwise noted, the other person then repeated the same words.)

MODERNIZED TRADITIONAL VOWS

It was important to Kristin and Josh that their vows were short and meaningful and that they incorporated a mix of contemporary and traditional elements.

Kristin/Josh: "I believe in you, the person you will grow to be and the couple we will be together. With my whole heart, I take you as my husband/wife, acknowledging and accepting your faults and strengths, as you do mine.

"I promise to be faithful and supportive and to always make our family's love and happiness my priority.

Melissa & Ben
CHICAGO, ILLINOIS
SEPTEMBER 4

Melissa is Catholic, and Ben is Jewish, so it was important to them to mix traditions that reflect both their heritages. They married under a huppah, read their ketubah aloud, and had the breaking of the glass as a nod to Ben's faith. To honor Melissa's background, the couple recited traditional Christian vows, lit a unity candle, and had readings from the Bible. The result? A deeply meaningful ceremony all their own.

"I will be yours in plenty and in want, in sickness and in health, in failure and in triumph.

"I will dream with you, celebrate with you, and walk beside you through whatever our lives may bring.

"You are my person—my love and my life, today and always."

NOSTALGIC VOWS

Anne and Mike wrote separate passages, as well as shared vows, to express their individual feelings to each other. They drew on moments that were reflective of their relationship, touching on a few milestones and inside jokes to keep it lighthearted.

Mike: "I love your smile, your kind heart, your adventurous spirit, your passion for learning new things, and for visiting new places.

"From river-rafting excursions, to volleyball on First Avenue, ski house weekends, relaxing evenings at the Writer's Hang, to whirlwind tours through the Swiss Alps, every moment of every day with you has been amazing.

"As we journey through this wonderful world, I take solace in knowing that my soul mate will be at my side every step of the way. To laugh during the good times, support each other through the turbulent times, and to love unconditionally at all times.

"Your energy and excitement are contagious. You inspire me to dream big and to live those dreams. You remind me to always enjoy life's pervading beauty."

Anne: "I used to think you weren't my type, but once we grew our friendship, I realized I didn't want someone that fit a 'type'; I wanted you—amazing, mold-breaking you. Your relentless energy, ambition, passion, camp-counselor spirit, Rosie the Riveter attitude, Boy Scout resourcefulness, and Mother Teresa heart all combine to make you the only man that is meant for me.

"You inspire me to think outside myself, dream big, not take flack from anyone, invent, bring together those we love, bring back the appendix, take the whole-fruit challenge, support the underdog, and always, always find the fun in life.

"I promise to be your co-adventurer, your ultimate support, and the one that makes you smile. I promise to encourage your passions, indulge your entrepreneurial spirit, and love you for exactly who you are. You are it, my cutes, there will be no one else, and I will honor and nurture that commitment with each and every day."

Mike and Anne's shared vows:

"On this day,
I give you my heart,
My promise,
That I will walk with you,
Hand in hand,
Wherever our journey leads us,
Living, learning, loving,
Together,
Forever."

FAMILY-CENTERED VOWS

Wanting to incorporate a few phrases from the vows that Andrea's parents had written for their own wedding, Andrea and Michael wrote these together, keeping them very similar, but with a few key differences.

Michael: "I choose you, Andrea, to be my wife, as my friend and love. I take you to be no other than yourself—loving what I know of you, and trusting what I do not. I make a commitment to you today that with God's help I will love and serve, honor and protect you. I promise to help shoulder our challenges, as there is nothing we cannot face if we stand together. I will walk with you in the sun and through any storm, and promise to keep myself for you alone as long as we both shall live. I love you."

Andrea: "I choose you, Michael, to be my husband, as my friend and love. I take you to be no other than yourself—loving what I know of you, and trusting what I do not. I make a commitment to you today that with God's help I will love and serve, honor and protect you. I promise to be your partner in all things, and to create with you a home that will truly be a portion of God's kingdom. I will walk with you in the sun and through any storm, and promise to keep myself for you alone as long as we both shall live. I love you."

INFORMAL VOWS

Kevin and Mai each wrote their vows separately, but they both ended up including lots of references to their shared love of travel.

Kevin: "I vow to love Mai for the rest of my life. I vow to value her, and honor her, until the end of my days. I vow to remember always my family and friends, and to return to them always, no matter how far we travel. I vow to remember what is truly valuable in life, and to value therefore the ones we spend it with. Mai, I love you so much I wake up sometimes and can hardly believe my luck for ever having met you. I promise to be your loving husband for the rest of my time on Earth."

Mai: "Kevin, you are my hero, my inspiration, my strength. Every day, without fail, you make me smile, and remind me how so lucky I am to have you in my life. Being with you has shown me how it is possible to love someone across oceans, time zones, and seasons. I vow to be your best friend, companion, and partner through life's ups and downs. I vow to grow together with you and love you more with each passing day. I promise to support you in your goals, to honor and respect you, and to always be there for you for as long as we both shall live. We have so many adventures ahead of us, and I look forward to taking each step by your side."

SHORT-AND-SWEET VOWS

Laine and Shane pieced together these promises based on traditional vows and fun lines. "We both thought they were perfect for our personalities and our relationship," Laine says.

"I promise to be your lover, companion and friend,
Your partner in parenthood,
Your ally in conflict,
Your greatest fan and your toughest adversary.
Your comrade in adventure,
Your student and your teacher,
Your consolation in disappointment,
Your accomplice in mischief,
This is my sacred vow to you, my equal in all things."

SIMPLE VOWS

Ted and Emily chose sections from vows that stood out to them and compiled them into a simple shared set of promises.

Ted/Emily: "I love you. You are my best friend.
Today I give myself to you in marriage.
I promise to encourage and inspire you, to laugh with you, and to comfort you in times of sorrow and struggle.
I promise to love you in good times and in bad, when life seems easy and when it seems hard, when our love is simple, and when it is an effort.

ASK CARLEY
FAMILY VOWS

How can we get our children involved in the ceremony?
Your kids are an important part of your new family—let them know it during your ceremony. Here are some great ways to make them feel a part of things:

- Do a family ring exchange. You and your partner give each other rings, and then the two of you present rings to the kids.

- Or give each child another piece of jewelry, like a wristwatch, cuff links, or a bracelet, after the two of you have exchanged vows and rings.

- Present kids with "family medallions" that bear the symbol of three joined circles—two for the couple and the third representing the child.

- Have the kids' "new" parent say vows to the children. An example:

"_____, I promise to accept and love you as my own and to protect and love you all of my life. I will to do my best to guide and support you." (You may add your own personal words—a few additional sentences—here.)

I promise to cherish you, and to always hold you in highest regard.
As we begin together this great adventure, these things
I promise to you today and all the days of our lives."

FUNNY VOWS

Dave and Stephanie dreamed up these humorous vows, keeping the tone light, but still sincere.

Dave: "I, Dave, take you, Stephanie, to be my wife, my partner in life, and my one true love. I will cherish our friendship and love you today, tomorrow, and until the day I die. I will always laugh with you and only occasionally at you. When I do laugh at you, if it is in public, I will do my best to create the illusion that it is with you.

"I promise to be there with you through the toughest of the trials in our life and to cry with you. These trials do not include things like YouTube footage of soldiers being reunited with their daughters. You're crying on your own with those.

"I vow to love you through the difficult and the easy. I promise to never put you or myself in danger. This means that I will never come between you and a mirror. I will also never force you to eat spicy food with me as I did on one of our first dates. I later found out that you were clenching your cheeks the whole night.

"What I admire most about you is your determination. But stamping your foot when you don't get your way is no longer cute after age nine. Seriously, you need to stop that.

"I look forward to being a married man and starting a new chapter in my life. For starters, I will no longer refer to it as 'my life,' but 'ours.' I look forward to being the best father I can be and helping you to be the best mother.

"This is my solemn vow to you today as I make you my wife."

Stephanie: "David, you make loving easy. For starters, you're the best roomie I've ever had. Living in sin, without our parents' blessings, was totally worth it. I now know you are able to deal with my annoying habits. And I've discovered that you have very few. You pick up my half-empty coffee cups that I leave around the house, you make me breakfast on the weekends, and you always know where my cell phone and keys are when I go into full panic mode and scream that someone stole them.

"With you I have learned to take it slow, although I could have dealt with getting to this altar a little faster. When we met, all I knew was that you made me laugh and you had a dorky look, which

I thought was hot. Only time would allow me to see your true colors. You're generous, loving, sensitive, kind, an insomniac, and a lover of daily man baths and boxer dogs.

"I promise with all my heart to love you when times are good and bad. When you're sore on Monday from sitting the same position all day during Sunday football, when men hit on you as you walk my Pomeranian, and when you need someone to lean on when work gets tough, I will always be your gal.

"When I'm scared, you make me feel safe. When I'm sad, you make me smile. There has yet to be a day where we haven't laughed together. I never want there to be one.

"I take you to be my husband, the father of my children, and best friend until death do us part. Just stay away for one week per month!"

LOVE LETTER VOWS

Adriana and Josh's rabbi asked the couple to each write an answer to the question "Why do you want to spend the rest of your life with Josh/Adriana?" The letters were read during the ceremony as vows.

Adriana: "I knew very early on after meeting you that I wanted to spend the rest of my life with you. That feeling has only grown stronger every day. Friends and family have asked me if I am nervous about getting married. I've never been nervous—not even for one instant of our engagement.

"I've never felt more certain of anything in my life. I love you for the person you are, and because of the way you make me feel. When I look at you, I know that I want to spend my life making you feel the same way.

"I think it is very rare to find someone in life who inspires you with their talent and ambition; who challenges you and shares so many interests with you; who, despite his intelligence, experience, and successes, has the humility, sensitivity, and selflessness to laugh with you, discover with you, and love you like you've never been loved before. I feel so lucky to have found that person in you, and I can't wait to start the rest of our lives together. If I could change one thing, it would only be for us to have met sooner. I know I will always be happy making you feel my love each and every day."

Josh: "When we met two and a half years ago, something happened. I had a feeling you were 'the one,' but for whatever reason, whether it was fear or insecurity, I was trapped in a world of singledom I could not escape. You, for some reason, stayed around long enough for me to figure it all out, and for that I owe you everything. About one year after we met, I knew it was over. I felt different, and now I had to make sure I would do everything right so you would feel the same way. Well, you did, and you gave me the greatest gift anyone could bestow on a companion. The gift to always want to be a better person for you! You inspire me, challenge me, make me laugh, keep me company, make me never want to be anywhere else but with you, and when I'm away, I just want to come home. You are my angel, and I love you. I will never again think in terms of 'I.' "

SAME-SEX VOWS

Anne and Gabrielle crafted their own meaningful vows that didn't follow typical wedding vow traditions.

"I take you, Gabrielle/Anne, to be my partner for life.
I promise above all else to live in truth with you
and to communicate fully and fearlessly.
I give you my hand and my heart
as a sanctuary of warmth and peace
and pledge my love, devotion, faith, and honor
as I join my life to yours."

TWIST ON TRADITIONAL VOWS

Dawn and David wrote vows that were said in conjunction with the traditional ones.

The couple's words:

"To my dearest Dawn/David,
Today is the day I give all of me to all of you.
On this day, I promise to support you mentally,
emotionally, and spiritually,
so that we may continually grow together as one.
On this day, I promise to be your confidant(e),
so that your heart may always be open to me.
On this day, I promise to offer you comfort in bad times,
so that we may be stronger in hours of need.
On this day, I promise to rejoice with you in good times,
so that we may know the blessing of sharing happiness.
Above all, on this day, I thank you for choosing me to love, support, comfort, and confide in,
and I thank God for allowing me to know the love that is within, and that is . . . you."

From the minister:

"I, David/Dawn, take you, Dawn/David,
to be my lawfully wedded wife/husband,
to come to this life filled with caring, honesty, and mutual respect.
I vow to love, honor, and cherish you
through all the changes of our lives,
for as long as we both shall live."

Dawn and David's wedding vows adapted from Jumping the Broom: The African-American Wedding Planner, *by Harriette Cole (Henry Holt, 1995), and* The Nubian Wedding Book: Words and Rituals to Celebrate and Plan an African-American Wedding, *by Ingrid Sturgis (Three Rivers Press, 1998)*

FREESTYLE VOWS

Vashia said the following vow to her husband, Lawrence, on their wedding day. As for Lawrence, "He did a freestyle verse the morning of the wedding that turned out to be a sermon," Vashia says. "I'd have to review the video-tape a billion times to get everything correct, verbatim!"

"Lawrence, Helen Keller has taught me that 'the best and most beautiful things in the world cannot be seen or even touched; they must be felt with the heart.' Now that we are beyond the romantic phase that every new couple endures, and our consciousness is no longer impaired, I see things clearly with both my heart and my head.

"Our relationship is ever growing and evolving, as any relationship striving for success will do. You and I are imperfect human beings in an imperfect world. Therefore, as much as society would like us to believe that love conquers all, you and I both know that that is a whimsical myth. With the world running at such a fast pace, there can be no marriage today without a conscious effort for tomorrow. Marriage is not self-sustaining. Marriage is not a nine-to-five job, but rather a corporation that requires nonstop nurturing. If we fail to labor in the vineyard, there will be no reward.

"Our union has been one of mind, heart, and spirit. Today we will be joined in body, making our union complete. On this day I make a covenant with you and the Creator. I know that together, with God as our center, we can reach any goal we envision.

"I, Vashia, take you, Lawrence, to be my husband, loving you in your growing and becoming. I will honor your goals and your dreams and help you to fulfill them. I shall stand by you in every success and failure you encounter. I will love you whether you are near or far, when you are at your best or at your worst; in times of joy and in times of sorrow. I say these things knowing that God is in the midst of them all. Lawrence, I am your wife from this day forward. I will walk with you all the days of my life."

JEWISH KETUBAH VOWS

For their vows, Robin and Adam read the text of their ketubah, the Jewish marriage contract, which they wrote based on the traditional model.

"Be my wife/husband according to the tradition of Moses and the people of Israel. I take you to be mine in love and friendship. I will nourish, respect, and support you with integrity and faithfulness. We stand under the huppah before family and friends to make a mutual covenant, becoming partners in marriage—loving and supportive companions in life. Together we will build a home, part of the community of Israel, guided by a reverence for the Divine and the laws, traditions, and ethics of our people. The symbols and rituals we cherish will forge a link to our heritage, a bond strengthened by learning, involvement, and acts of loving kindness.

"Should we be blessed to raise children, we will give them a loving home and share with them a deep appreciation for our history and culture. We will be linked eternally to the history of our ancestors and the future of the Jewish people. We, as beloveds and friends, will develop our lives individually and together, responsible to and for each other. We will fill our lives with laughter and affection. We will encourage each other's music and writing. Together, we will support each other's intellectual, emotional, spiritual, and creative fulfillment.

"We declare that just as this is a permanent joining of our two lives, so it also constitutes a joining of material substance and worth. Through marriage we assume the responsibility to support each other and our family. If we should part, we promise to act with concern and compassion for the physical, economic, and emotional needs of each other and those whose lives are intertwined with ours. Joyfully we enter into this covenant of marriage, and we solemnly accept its obligations. It is valid and binding."

2
readings

*Love—along with birth and death—*is probably the most written-about topic in human history. Writers through the centuries have philosophized about, pondered over, raged against, and swooned before the idea of love, and they have done so in so many unique, beautiful, and inspiring ways that you'll have countless choices for wedding readings. From Scripture to Shakespeare to the poetry of E. E. Cummings or Pablo Neruda, chances are some scribe has perfectly articulated the feelings you want to express on your wedding day.

BECOMING WELL READ

With all the wonderful words of the world's greatest writers out there at your disposal, how do you choose the ones that mean the most to the two of you, who should read these dear words, and when in the ceremony they should be included? Begin by asking yourselves some questions.

what to select?

- If you feel an affinity for a certain poet, if you've never forgotten the passage about Cathy and Heathcliff's love in *Wuthering Heights* (which you first read in high school), or if your fiancé presented you with a copy of Shakespeare's sonnets on your first Christmas together, including such readings in your ceremony is priceless.

- If you're having a religious ceremony, there may be certain requirements about or restrictions on what can be read. Your officiant may give you a list of approved pieces of Scripture to choose from.

- If you're looking for a way to honor a deceased or absent parent, reading one of their favorite poems or pieces of prose or Scripture is appropriate. Reading excerpts of an old letter written during their life is another moving option.

- Readings are a wonderful way to place your wedding in a period. If you're planning a celebration with a medieval or a Victorian flair, choose poems and passages from those times.

- Feel free to use ethnic or cultural readings that don't necessarily reflect your backgrounds—what's important is that the words resonate for you. Do explain the reading's source in the program or introduction—for example, "an Aztec marriage poem."

- If you find many very short passages that you really like, consider having multiple readers recite them one after the other, with each person being introduced before he or she reads (like the Jewish Seven Blessings; see page 50).

- A song is just a poem put to music—your favorite lyrics may make a great selection.

- Do you have a piece you really adore, but don't trust anyone else to perform as brilliantly as you would? Be a reader yourself, or encourage your partner to read. Or read to each other and surprise your new spouse with your selection.

- Sometimes couples choose a reader but leave the choice of the reading up to him or her. Make sure your readers clear their selections with your officiant to avoid any faux pas.

- You or your partner may be moved to write something original for the ceremony—a poem, perhaps. Either read it yourself, or ask a close friend or relative to do so.

- Keep in mind that passages from wedding readings can also be used in toasts, or as quotes to grace your invitations or programs. (See page 113 for more ideas.)

who reads?

- You may want to choose friends and relatives whom you wish to involve in the ceremony in some way but who are not in the wedding party. Parents and grandparents can read as well. Ask readers well ahead of time to participate—at least four months before the wedding—and if they aren't choosing their own selections, give them a copy of what they'll be reading, so they can practice. And do be gracious if they decline. Public speaking is the number one fear of most Americans!

- Prep your readers ahead of time. Have them take a cue from broadcast journalists and print out their text on index cards, have it prepared on a tablet, or even handwritten in a beautiful journal. You don't want your reader up there holding crumpled scraps of paper.

- You may want to ask your officiant to introduce each reader as his or her cue ("And now Elizabeth, the bride's friend, will read a passage from _____ ."). Not only will your readers not have the extra stress of worrying about when it's time to stand up, but all your guests will know each person's significance to you.

- People tend to get nervous and start speaking too quickly. Reassure your readers that there is plenty of time for them to read, so they should try to speak slowly and clearly (and remember to breathe!).

- Make sure each reader gives the title and author (and significance, if appropriate) of the piece before starting to read. Also put this information in your ceremony program, if you'll have one.

- Some of the readings listed here or that you'll find elsewhere may have a specific gender bent—that is, they may extol the beauty of a lady from a man's point of view. You'll want to make sure that something like that is read by an appropriate person—a male reader, if not the groom himself.

feel young again

Look to children's literature for sweet, fun readings.

- *The Complete Poems of Winnie-the-Pooh*, by A. A. Milne (Dutton Books, 1998)

- *Corduroy*, by Don Freeman (Viking Press, 1985)

- *The Giving Tree*, by Shel Silverstein (Harper Collins Juvenile Books, 1986)

- *Guess How Much I Love You*, by Sam McBratney (Candlewick Press, 1995)

- *I Like You*, by Sandol Stoddard Warburg (Houghton Mifflin, 1990)

- *The Little Prince*, by Antoine de Saint-Exupéry (Harcourt Brace, 1968)

- *Made for Each Other*, by William Steig (Harper-Collins Juvenile Books, 2000)

- *The Velveteen Rabbit*, by Margery Williams Bianco (Doubleday, 1958)

- *What the Dormouse Said: Lessons for Grown-ups from Children's Books*, compiled by Amy Gash (Algonquin Books, 1999)

- *Should I Share My Ice Cream?*, by Mo Willems (Hyperion, 2011)

how's it done?

- Readings are usually interspersed throughout the ceremony. You might plan one right after the greeting, another after your vows but before the ring exchange, and one to close the ceremony, before the recessional music. Talk to your officiant about exactly how things will flow; he or she may leave it up to you or may have a specific ceremony order he or she usually follows.

- Depending on how large your wedding is, readers may be able to remain standing at their seat to read, or they may need to come up to the stage or altar and read into a microphone. (They should all be invited to the rehearsal to go over the ceremony order and their place in it.)

- There's no set time limit on readings, but in the interest of short attention spans, make sure they're not too long. A simple poem can be read in less than a minute in most cases; a piece of prose may take several more. (You might want to excerpt the most significant passages from a longer piece instead of having someone read the entire thing.) Four or five minutes tops is probably more than enough time for the readers to express the sentiment for which you chose the piece.

- Have copies of the readings to hand out if you aren't having a program. Wrapped in a nice way, these make a great favor. For example, you could have them printed on nice parchment paper, rolled into a scroll, and tied with a ribbon. Place them at your guests' place settings, or at least set them out in baskets for guests to take as they leave the ceremony site.

TRADITIONAL RELIGIOUS READINGS

Religious texts are the source of some of the most beautiful verses on the subject of marriage. Even if you are having a secular or nontraditional ceremony, consider using any of the following passages.

scripture

Please note that couples marrying in the Catholic Church should choose their readings from a prescribed list, which does not include all the selections listed below but does include additional texts.

OLD TESTAMENT

The lord God said: "It is not good for the man to be alone. I will make a suitable partner for him." So the lord God formed out of the ground various wild animals and various birds of the air, and he brought them to the man to see what he would call them; whatever the man called each of them would be its name. The man gave names to all the cattle, all the birds of the air, and all the wild animals; but none proved to be the suitable partner for the man.

So the lord God cast a deep sleep on the man, and while he was asleep, he took out one of his ribs and closed up the place with flesh. The lord God then built up into a woman the rib that he had taken from the man. When he brought her to the man, the man said:

"This one, at last, is bone of my bones
and flesh of my flesh;
This one shall be called 'woman,'
for out of 'her man' this one has been taken."

That is why a man leaves his father and mother and clings to his wife, and the two of them become one body.

—Genesis 2:18–24

Go, eat your bread with joy and drink your wine with a merry heart, because it is now that God favors your works. At all times let your garments be white, and spare not the perfume for your head. Enjoy life with the wife whom you love, all the days of the fleeting life that is granted you under the sun. This is your lot in life, for the toil of your labors under the sun.

—Ecclesiastes 9:7–9

So I will allure her;
I will lead her into the desert
and speak to her heart.
From there I will give her the vineyards she had,
and the valley of Achor as a door of hope.
She shall respond there as in the days of her youth,
when she came up from the land of Egypt.
On that day, says the lord,
She shall call me "My husband."

I will espouse you to me forever:
I will espouse you in right and in justice,
in love and in mercy;

I will espouse you in fidelity,
and you shall know the lord.

—*Hosea 2:14–16; 19–20*

NEW TESTAMENT

This is my commandment: love one another as I have loved you. There is
no greater love than this: to lay down one's life for one's friends. . . .
It was not you who chose me, it was I who chose you to go forth and
bear fruit. Your fruit must endure, so that all you ask the Father in my
name he will give you. The command I give you is this, that you love one
another.

—*John 15:12–13; 16–17*

Your love must be sincere. Detest what is evil, cling to what is good.
Love one another with the affection of brothers. Anticipate each other
in showing respect. Do not grow slack but be fervent in spirit; he whom
you serve is the lord. Rejoice in hope, be patient under trial, persevere
in prayer. Look on the needs of the saints as your own; be generous in
offering hospitality. Bless your persecutors; bless and do not curse them.
Rejoice with those who rejoice, weep with those who weep. Have the
same attitude toward all. Put away ambitious thoughts and associate
with those who are lowly. Do not be wise in your own estimation. Never
repay injury with injury. See that your conduct is honorable in the eyes
of all. If possible, live peaceably with everyone.

Romans 12:9–18

If I speak with human tongues and angelic as well, but do not have love,
I am a noisy gong, a clanging cymbal. If I have the gift of prophecy, and,
with full knowledge, comprehend all mysteries, if I have faith great
enough to move mountains, but have not love, I am nothing. If I give
everything I have to feed the poor and hand over my body to be burned,
but have not love, I gain nothing.

Love is patient; love is kind. Love is not jealous, it does not put on
airs, it is not snobbish. Love is never rude, it is not self-seeking, it is not
prone to anger; neither does it brood over injuries. Love does not rejoice
in what is wrong but rejoices with the truth. There is no limit to love's
forbearance, to its trust, its hope, its power to endure.

Love never fails. Prophecies will cease, tongues will be silent,
knowledge will pass away. . . . There are in the end three things that
last: faith, hope, and love, and the greatest of these is love.

—*1 Corinthians 13:1–8; 13*

responsorial psalms

Christian ceremonies usually include a responsorial psalm; you may be able to have close friends and relatives contribute by leading the response (usually the first line of the psalm or another well-known line in it) or by reciting the verses, or your officiant may have a church official do so. Here are a few possibilities; look at the Book of Psalms or talk to your officiant for more ideas.

I

I will bless the LORD at all times;
   his praise shall be ever in my mouth.
Let my soul glory in the LORD;
   the lowly will hear me and be glad.
Glorify the LORD with me,
   let us together extol his name.

II

I sought the LORD, and he answered me
   and delivered me from all my fears.
Look to him that you may be radiant with joy,
   and your faces may not blush with shame.

III

Come, children, hear me;
   I will teach you the fear of the LORD.
Which of you desires life,
   and takes delight in prosperous days?
Keep your tongue from evil
   and your lips from speaking guile;
Turn from evil, and do good;
   seek peace, and follow after it.
The LORD has eyes for the just,
   and ears for their cry.
The LORD confronts the evildoers,
   to destroy remembrance of them from the earth.
When the just cry out, the LORD hears them,
   and from all their distress he rescues them.
   —From Psalm 34

Sing joyfully to the LORD, all you lands;
   serve the LORD with gladness;
   come before him with joyful song.
Know that the LORD is God;
   he made us, his we are;
   his people, the flock he tends.
Enter his gates with thanksgiving,
   his courts with praise;

Give thanks to him; bless his name, for he is good:
   the LORD, whose kindness endures forever,
   and his faithfulness, to all generations.
   —Psalm 100

I

Give thanks to the LORD, for he is good,
   for his mercy endures forever;
Give thanks to the God of gods,
   for his mercy endures forever;
Give thanks to the LORD of lords,
   for his mercy endures forever;

II

Who alone does great wonders,
   for his mercy endures forever;
Who made the heavens in wisdom,
   for his mercy endures forever;
Who spread out the earth upon the waters,
   for his mercy endures forever;
Who made the great lights,
   for his mercy endures forever;
The sun to rule over the day,
   for his mercy endures forever;
The moon and the stars to rule over the night,
   for his mercy endures forever.
   —From Psalm 136

Praise the LORD in his sanctuary,
   praise him in the firmament of his strength.
Praise him for his mighty deeds,
   praise him for his sovereign majesty.
Praise him with the blast of the trumpet,
   praise him with lyre and harp,
Praise him with timbrel and dance,
   praise him with strings and pipe.
Praise him with sounding cymbals,
   praise him with clanging cymbals.
Let everything that has breath
   praise the LORD! Alleluia.
   —Psalm 150

That is why I kneel before the Father from whom every family in heaven and on earth takes its name; and I pray that he will bestow on you gifts in keeping with the riches of his glory. May he strengthen you inwardly through the working of his Spirit. May Christ dwell in your hearts through faith, and may charity be the root and foundation of your life. Thus you will be able to grasp fully, and with all the holy ones, the breadth and length and height and depth of Christ's love, and experience this love which surpasses all knowledge, so that you may attain to the fullness of God himself.

—*Ephesians 3:14–19*

Because you are God's chosen ones, holy and beloved, clothe yourselves with heartfelt mercy, with kindness, humility, meekness, and patience. Bear with one another; forgive whatever grievances you have against one another. Forgive as the lord has forgiven you. Over all these virtues put on love, which binds the rest together and makes them perfect. Christ's peace must reign in your hearts, since as members of the one body you have been called to that peace. Dedicate yourselves to thankfulness. Let the word of Christ, rich as it is, dwell in you. In wisdom made perfect, instruct and admonish one another. Sing gratefully to God from your hearts in psalms, hymns, and inspired songs. Whatever you do, whether in speech or in action, do it in the name of the Lord Jesus. Give thanks to God the Father through him.

—*Colossians 3:12–17*

Beloved, let us love one another because love is of God; everyone who loves is begotten of God and has knowledge of God. The man without love has known nothing of God, for God is love. God's love was revealed in our midst in this way: he sent his only Son to the world that we might have life through him. Love, then, consists in this: not that we have loved God, but that he has loved us and has sent his Son as an offering for our sins.

Beloved, if God has loved us so, we must have the same love for one another. No one has ever seen God. Yet if we love one another God dwells in us, and his love is brought to perfection in us.

We have come to know and to believe in the love God has for us. God is love, and he who abides in love abides in God, and God in him. . . .

Love has no room for fear; rather, perfect love casts out all fear. And since fear has to do with punishment, love is not yet perfect in one who is afraid. We, for our part, love because he first loved us.

—*1 John 4:7–12; 16; 18–19*

Listen! My beloved! Behold, he is coming, Climbing on the mountains, Leaping on the hills!

My beloved is like a gazelle or a young stag. Behold, he is standing behind our wall, He is looking through the windows, He is peering through the lattice.

My beloved responded and said to me, "Arise, my darling, my beautiful one, And come along."

For behold, the winter is past, The rain is over and gone.
The flowers have already appeared in the land; The time has arrived for pruning the vines, And the voice of the turtledove has been heard in our land.

The fig tree has ripened its figs, And the vines in blossom have given forth their fragrance. Arise, my darling, my beautiful one, And come along!

O my dove, in the clefts of the rock, In the secret place of the steep pathway, Let me see your form, Let me hear your voice; For your voice is sweet, And your form is lovely.

Catch the foxes for us, The little foxes that are ruining the vineyards, While our vineyards are in blossom.

My beloved is mine, and I am his; He pastures his flock among the lilies.
—*Song of Solomon, 2:8–16*

Set me as a seal on your heart,
as a seal on your arm;
For stern as death is love,
relentless as the nether world is devotion;
its flames are a blazing fire.
Deep waters cannot quench love,
nor floods sweep it away.
Were one to offer all he owns to purchase love,
he would be roundly mocked.
—*Song of Songs (Song of Solomon) 8:6–7*

the jewish seven blessings (sheva b'rachot)

The seven Jewish wedding blessings praise God for creating the fruit of the vine (wine); humankind; man and woman; the miracle of childbirth; bringing the bride and groom together like the first couple, Adam and Eve; the couple's joy and the hope for a future filled with their joy; and the voices of their children. Usually couples choose seven relatives and friends to recite them.

We have chosen an egalitarian translation of the seven blessings. There are many different versions; please consult your rabbi regarding the best translation to use in your ceremony.

Blessed are You, Adonai our God, Source of the universe, who created the fruit of the vine, symbol of joy.

Blessed are You, Adonai our God, Source of the universe, who has created all things to Your glory.

Blessed are You, Adonai our God, Source of the universe, Creator of humankind.

Blessed are You, Adonai our God, Source of the universe, who has made man in Your image after Your likeness, and has fashioned woman from man as his companion, that together they may perpetuate life. Blessed are You, Adonai, Creator of humankind.

May Zion rejoice as her children are restored to her in joy. Blessed are You, Adonai, who causes Zion to rejoice at her children's return.

Make this bride and groom into loving companions, just as You did the creatures in the Garden of Eden. Blessed are You, Adonai, who bestows lasting joy on groom and bride.

Blessed are You, Adonai our God, Source of the universe, who has created joy and gladness, bride and groom, mirth and exultation, pleasure and delight, love and friendship, peace and fellowship. May we all see the day when the sounds of joy fill the streets of Jerusalem and echo throughout the world, as the voices of the groom and the bride, the jubilant voices of those joined in marriage under the bridal canopy, and of youths feasting and singing. Blessed are You, Adonai, who rejoices with the bride and groom.

buddhist marriage homily

Nothing happens without a cause. The union of this man and woman has not come about accidentally but is the foreordained result of many past lives. This tie can therefore not be broken or resolved.

In the future, happy occasions will come as surely as the morning. Difficult times will come as surely as night. When things go joyously, meditate according to the Buddhist tradition. When things go badly, meditate. Meditation in the manner of the Compassionate Buddha will guide your life.

To say the words *love* and *compassion* is easy. But to accept that love and compassion are built upon patience and perseverance is not easy. Your marriage will be firm and lasting if you remember this.

CULTURAL READINGS AND BLESSINGS

I know not whether thou has been absent:
I lie down with thee, I rise up with thee,
In my dreams thou art with me.
If my eardrops tremble in my ears,
I know it is thou moving within my heart.
—*Aztec love song*

☐ LOVE IT ☐ LIKE IT

Let the earth of my body be mixed with the earth
my beloved walks on.
Let the fire of my body be the brightness
in the mirror that reflects his face.
Let the water of my body join the waters
of the lotus pool he bathes in.
Let the breath of my body be air
lapping his tired limbs.
Let me be sky, and moving through me
the cloud-dark Shyama, my beloved.
—*Hindu love poem*

☐ LOVE IT ☐ LIKE IT

LOVE IT   LIKE IT

Rising Sun! when you shall shine,
Make this house happy,
Beautify it with your beams;
Make this house happy,
God of Dawn! your white blessings spread;
Make this house happy.
Guard the doorway from all evil;
Make this house happy.
White corn! Abide herein;
Make this house happy.
Soft wealth! May this hut cover much;
Make this house happy.
Heavy Rain! Your virtues send;
Make this house happy.
Corn Pollen! Bestow content;
Make this house happy.
May peace around this family dwell;
Make this house happy.

—*Navajo chant*

LOVE IT   LIKE IT

You are my husband/wife.
My legs run because of you.
My feet dance because of you.
My heart shall beat because of you.
My eyes see because of you.
My mind thinks because of you.
And I shall love because of you.

—*Eskimo love song*

LOVE IT   LIKE IT

In our next life,
We will be birds flying wing to wing in the sky,
Or sturdy branches entangled with each other on the earth.

—*Bai Ju-yi*
Tang Dynasty, China
Translation by Richard Liu

LOVE IT   LIKE IT

Fair is the white star of twilight, and the sky clearer at the
day's end;
But she is fairer, and she is dearer,
She, my heart's friend.
Fair is the white star of twilight, and the moon roving to the
sky's end;

But she is fairer, better worth loving,
She, my heart's friend.

—*Traditional Shoshone love poem*

God in heaven above please protect the ones we love.
We honor all you created as we pledge our hearts and lives together.
We honor mother earth—and ask for our marriage to be abundant and
    grow stronger through the seasons;
We honor fire—and ask that our union be warm and glowing with love
    in our hearts;
We honor wind—and ask that we sail through life safe and calm as in
    our father's arms;
We honor water—to clean and soothe our relationship, that it may never
    thirst for love;
With all the forces of the universe you created, we pray for harmony
and true happiness as we forever grow young together.

—*Cherokee prayer*

☐ LOVE IT   ☐ LIKE IT

Live in joy, In love,
Even among those who hate.

Live in joy, In health,
Even among the afflicted.

Live in joy, In peace,
Even among the troubled.

Look within. Be still.
Free from fear and attachment,
Know the sweet joy of living in the way.

There is no fire like greed,
No crime like hatred,
No sorrow like separation,
No sickness like hunger of heart,
And no joy like the joy of freedom.

Health, contentment and trust
Are your greatest possessions,
And freedom your greatest joy.

Look within. Be still.
Free from fear and attachment,
Know the sweet joy of living in the way.

—*From the Dhammapada (Buddhist scripture)*

☐ LOVE IT   ☐ LIKE IT

These are the hands of your best friend, young and strong and full of love for you, that are holding yours on your wedding day, as you promise to love each other today, tomorrow, and forever. These are the hands that will work alongside yours, as together you build your future. These are the hands that will passionately love you and cherish you through the years, and with the slightest touch, will comfort you like no other. These are the hands that will hold you when fear or grief fills your mind. These are the hands that will countless times wipe the tears from your eyes; tears of sorrow, and as in today, tears of joy. These are the hands that will tenderly hold your children, the hands that will help you to hold your family as one. These are the hands that will give you strength when you need it. And lastly, these are the hands that even when wrinkled and aged, will still be reaching for yours, still giving you the same unspoken tenderness with just a touch.

—*Modern marriage blessing*

POETRY AND PROSE

From "Poem 1"

—*Sappho, seventh century BCE*

Come to me now once again and release me
from grueling anxiety.
All that my heart longs for,
fulfill. And be yourself my ally in love's battle.

The Couple's Tao Te Ching: "See Clearly"

—*Lao Tzu, sixth century BCE*
Reinterpreted by William Martin

Your love is a great mystery.
It is like an eternal lake
whose waters are always still and clear like glass.
Looking into it you can see
the truth about your life.

It is like a deep well
whose waters are cool and pure.
Drinking from it you can be reborn.

You do not have to stir the waters
or dig the well.
Merely see yourself clearly
And drink deeply.

The Couple's Tao Te Ching: "Always Return"

—Lao Tzu, sixth century BCE
Reinterpreted by William Martin

It is good to know your strength
but always return to your flexibility.
If you can cradle your beloved in your arms
in nurturing gentleness,
love will flow through you.

It is good to achieve things
but always return to anonymity.
Your beloved does not need your achievements
but needs your uncomplicated soul.
. . .
It is good to work for change,
but always return to what is.
If you accept all things whether painful or joyful,
you will always know
that you belong to each other
and to the Tao.

The Couple's Tao Te Ching: "A Sacred Space"

—Lao Tzu, sixth century BCE
Reinterpreted by William Martin

Your love requires space in which to grow.
This space must be safe enough
to allow your hearts to be revealed.
It must offer refreshment for your spirits
and renewal for your minds.
It must be a space made sacred
by the quality of your honesty,
attention, love, and compassion.
It may be anywhere,
inside or out,
but it must exist.

LOVE IT LIKE IT

The Couple's Tao Te Ching: "Transforming Power"

—Lao Tzu, sixth century BCE
Reinterpreted by William Martin

Your love contains the power
of a thousand suns.
It unfolds as naturally and effortlessly
as does a flower,
and graces the world with its blooming.
Its beauty radiates a transforming energy
that enlivens all who see it.
Because of you, compassion and joy
are added to the world.
That is why the stars sing together
because of your love.

LOVE IT LIKE IT

"Blessing the Marriage"

—Rumi, thirteenth century
Translated by Coleman Barks with A. J. Arberry

This marriage be wine with halvah, honey dissolving in milk.
This marriage be the leaves and fruit of a date tree.
This marriage be women laughing together for days on end.
This marriage, a sign for us to study.
This marriage, beauty.
This marriage, a moon in a light blue sky.
This marriage, this silence fully mixed with spirit.

LOVE IT LIKE IT

"In Love That Long"

—Rumi, thirteenth century
Translated by Coleman Barks

I am here, this moment, inside the beauty,
the gift God has given,
Our love:
This gold and circular sign
means we are free of any duty:
out of eternity
I turn my face to you, and into
eternity:
We have been in
love that long.

From *The Divine Comedy*

—*Dante Alighieri, thirteenth to fourteenth century*

The love of God, unutterable and perfect, flows into a pure soul the way light rushes into a transparent object. The more love we receive, the more love we shine forth; so that, as we grow clear and open, the more complete the joy of loving is. And the more souls who resonate together, the greater the intensity of their love, for, mirror-like, each soul reflects the other.

"Married Love"

—*Kuan Tao-shêng, thirteenth century*
Translated by Kenneth Rexroth and Ling Chung

You and I
Have so much love,
That it
Burns like a fire,
In which we bake a lump of clay
Molded into a figure of you
And a figure of me.
Then we take both of them,
And break them into pieces,
And mix the pieces with water,
And mold again a figure of you,
And a figure of me.
I am in your clay.
You are in my clay.
In life we share a single quilt.
In death we will share one coffin.

"My True Love Hath My Heart"

—*Sir Philip Sidney, sixteenth century*

My true love hath my heart and I have his,
By just exchange, one for another given;
I hold his dear, and mine he cannot miss;
There never was a better bargain driven.
My heart in me keeps him and me in one;
My heart in him his thoughts and senses guides;
He loves my heart, for once it was his own;
I cherish his, because in me it bides.
My true love hath my heart and I have his.

"The Passionate Shepherd to His Love"

—Christopher Marlowe, sixteenth century

Come live with me and be my love,
And we will all the pleasures prove
That hills and valleys, dales and fields
And all the craggy mountains yields.

There we will sit upon the rocks
And see the shepherds feed their flocks,
By shallow rivers to whose falls
Melodious birds sing madrigals.

And I will make thee beds of roses
With a thousand fragrant posies
A cap of flowers and a kirtle
Embroidered all with leaves of myrtle.

A gown made of the finest wool
Which from our pretty lambs we pull;
Fair lined slippers for the cold,
With buckles of the purest gold;

A belt of straw and ivy buds,
With coral clasps and amber studs:
And if these pleasure may thee move,
Come live with me and be my love.

The shepherds' swains shall dance and sing
For thy delight each May morning:
If these delights thy mind may move,
Then live with me and be my love.

"So Well I Love Thee"

—Michael Drayton, sixteenth to seventeenth century

So well I love thee, as without thee I
Love nothing; if I might choose, I'd rather die
Than be one day debarr'd thy company.

. . .

Since beasts, and plants do grow, and live and move,
Beasts are those men, that such a life approve,
He only lives, that deadly is in love.

The corn that in the ground is sown first dies
And of one seed do many ears arise:
Love, this world's corn, by dying multiplies.

The seeds of love first by thy eyes were thrown
Into a ground untill'd, a heart unknown
To bear such fruit, till by thy hands 'twas sown.

Look as your looking-glass by chance may fall,
Divide and break in many pieces small
And yet shows forth the selfsame face in all:

Proportions, features, graces just the same,
And in the smallest piece as well the name
Of fairest one deserves, as in the richest frame.

So all my thoughts are pieces but of you
Which put together makes a glass so true
As I therein no other's face but yours can view.

Sonnet XVIII

—William Shakespeare, sixteenth to seventeenth century

☐ LOVE IT ☐ LIKE IT

Shall I compare thee to a summer's day?
Thou art more lovely and more temperate:
Rough winds do shake the darling buds of May,
And summer's lease hath all too short a date:
Sometimes too hot the eye of heaven shines,
And often is his gold complexion dimm'd,
And every fair from fair sometime declines,
By chance, or nature's changing course, untrim'd,
But thy eternal summer shall not fade,
Nor loose possession of that fair thou ow'st,
Nor shall death brag thou wandr'st in his shade,
When in eternal lines to time thou gro'st,
So long as men can breathe, or eyes can see,
So long lives this, and this gives life to thee.

LOVE IT LIKE IT

Sonnet CXVI

—William Shakespeare, sixteenth to seventeenth century

Let me not to the marriage of true minds
Admit impediments. Love is not love
Which alters when it alteration finds,
Or bends with the remover to remove:
O, no! It is an ever-fixed mark,
That looks on tempests and is never shaken;
It is the star to every wandering bark,
Whose worth's unknown, although his height be taken.
Love's not Time's fool, though rosy lips and cheeks
Within his bending sickle's compass come;
Love alters not with his brief hours and weeks,
But bears it out even to the edge of doom.
If this is error, and upon me prov'd,
I never writ, nor no man ever lov'd.

LOVE IT LIKE IT

From *Paradise Lost*

—John Milton, seventeenth century

That what seemed fair in all the world seemed now
Mean, or in her summed up, in her contained,
And in her looks, which from that time infused
Sweetness into my heart, unfelt before,
And into all things from her air inspired
The spirit of love and amorous delight.

When I approach
Her loveliness, so absolute she seems,
And in herself complete, so well to know
Her own, that what she wills to do or say
Seems wisest, virtuousest, discreetest, best;
All higher knowledge in her presence falls
Degraded, wisdom in discourse with her
Loses discountenance, and like folly shows.

"She Walks in Beauty"

—Lord Byron, nineteenth century

She walks in beauty, like the night
Of cloudless climes and starry skies;
And all that's best of dark and bright
Meet in her aspect and her eyes:
Thus mellow'd to that tender light
Which heaven to gaudy day denies.

One shade the more, one ray the less,
Had half impair'd the nameless grace
Which waves in every raven tress,
Or softly lightens o'er her face;
Where thoughts serenely sweet express
How pure, how dear their dwelling-place.

And on that cheek, and o'er that brow,
So soft, so calm, yet eloquent,
The smiles that win, the tints that glow,
But tell of days in goodness spent,
A mind at peace with all below,
A heart whose love is innocent!

Sonnet XIV

—Elizabeth Barrett Browning
From Sonnets from the Portuguese, *nineteenth century*

If thou must love me, let it be for nought
Except for love's sake only. Do not say,
"I love her for her smile—her look—her way
Of speaking gently,—for a trick of thought
That falls in well with mine, and certes brought
A sense of pleasant ease on such a day."—
For these things in themselves, Beloved, may
Be changed, or change for thee,—and love, so wrought,
May be unwrought so. Neither love me for
Thine own dear pity's wiping my cheeks dry,—
A create might forget to weep, who bore
Thy comfort long, and lose thy love thereby!
But love me for love's sake, that evermore
Thou may best love on, through love's eternity.

Sonnet XLIII

—Elizabeth Barrett Browning
From Sonnets from the Portuguese, *nineteenth century*

How do I love thee? Let me count the ways.
I love thee to the depth and breadth and height
My soul can reach, when feeling out of sight
For the ends of Being and ideal Grace.
I love thee to the level of everyday's
Most quiet need, by sun and candlelight.
I love thee freely, as men strive for Right;
I love thee purely, as they turn from Praise.
I love thee with the passion put to us
In my old griefs, and with my childhood's faith.
I love thee with a love I seemed to lose
With my lost saints,—I love thee with the breath,
Smiles, tears, of all my life!—and, if God choose,
I shall but love thee better after death.

Sonnet XII

—Elizabeth Barrett Browning
From Sonnets from the Portuguese, *nineteenth century*

Indeed this very love which is my boast,
And which, when rising up from breast to brow,
Doth crown me with a ruby large enow
To draw men's eyes and prove the inner cost—
This love even, all my worth, to the uttermost,
I should not love withal, unless that thou
Hadst set me an example, shown me how,
When first thine earnest eyes with mine were crossed,
And love called love. And thus, I cannot speak
Of love even, as a good thing of my own:
Thy soul hath snatched up mine all faint and weak,
And places it by thee on a golden throne—
And that I love (O soul, we must be meek!)
Is by thee only whom I love alone.

"Believe Me, If All Those Endearing Young Charms"

—Thomas Moore, nineteenth century

LOVE IT   LIKE IT

Believe me, if all those endearing young charms,
Which I gaze on so fondly today,
Were to change by to-morrow, and fleet in my arms,
Like fairy-gifts fading away,
Thou wouldst still be adored, as this moment thou art,
Let thy loveliness fade as it will,
And around the dear ruin each wish of my heart
Would entwine itself verdantly still.

It is not while beauty and youth are thine own,
And thy cheeks unprofaned by a tear,
That the fervor and faith of a soul may be known,
To which time will but make thee more dear!
No, the heart that has truly loved never forgets,
But as truly loves on to the close,
As the sunflower turns to her god when he sets
The same look which she turned when he rose!

"A Birthday"

—Christina Rossetti, nineteenth century

LOVE IT   LIKE IT

My heart is like a singing bird
Whose nest is in a watered shoot;
My heart is like an apple-tree
Whose boughs are bent with thick-set fruit;
My heart is like a rainbow shell
That paddles in a halcyon sea,
My heart is gladder than all these,
Because my love is come to me.

Raise me a dais of silk and down;
Hang it with vair and purple dyes;
Carve it in doves and pomegranates,
And peacocks with a hundred eyes;
Work it in gold and silver grapes,
In leaves and silver fleur-de-lys;
Because the birthday of my life
Is come, my love is come to me.

"Love"

—Christina Rossetti, nineteenth century

What is the beginning? Love.
What is the course. Love still.
What the goal. The goal is love.
On a happy hill.
Is there nothing then but love?
Search we sky or earth
There is nothing out of Love
Hath perpetual worth:
All things flag but only Love,
All things fail and flee;
There is nothing left but Love
Worthy you and me.

From *Wuthering Heights*

—Emily Brontë, nineteenth century

. . . He's more myself than I am. Whatever our souls are made of, his and mine are the same. . . . If all else perished and he remained, I should still continue to be, and if all else remained, and he were annihilated, the universe would turn to a mighty stranger. . . . He's always, always in my mind; not as a pleasure to myself, but as my own being.

From *Jane Eyre*

—Charlotte Brontë, nineteenth century

I have for the first time found what I can truly love—I have found you. You are my sympathy—my better self—my good angel—I am bound to you with a strong attachment. I think you good, gifted, lovely: a fervent, a solemn passion is conceived in my heart; it leans to you, draws you to my centre and spring of life, wraps my existence about you—and, kindling in pure, powerful flame, fuses you and me in one.

"Love Is Enough"

—William Morris, nineteenth century

Love is enough: though the World be a-waning,
And the woods have no voice but the voice of complaining,
Though the sky be too dark for dim eyes to discover

The gold-cups and daisies fair blooming thereunder,
Though the hills be held shadows, and the sea a dark wonder
And this day draw a veil over all deeds passed over,
Yet their hands shall not tremble, their feet shall not falter;
The void shall not weary, the fear shall not alter
These lips and these eyes of the loved and the lover.

From "Give All to Love"

—*Ralph Waldo Emerson, nineteenth century*

Give all to love;
Obey thy heart;
Friends, kindred, days
Estate, good-fame,
Plans, credit and the Muse,
Nothing refuse.

'Tis a brave master;
Let it have scope:
Follow it utterly,
Hope beyond hope:
High and more high
It dives into noon,
With wing unspent,
Untold intent;
But it is a god,
Knows its own path
And the outlets of the sky.

It was never for the mean;
It requireth courage stout.
Souls above doubt,
Valour unbending.
It will reward,
They shall return
More than they were,
And ever ascending.

LOVE IT   LIKE IT

From "Song of the Open Road"

—Walt Whitman, nineteenth century

Listen! I will be honest with you. I do not offer the old
smooth prizes, but I offer rough new prizes.

These are the days that must happen to you:
You shall not heap up what is called riches,
You shall scatter with lavish hand all that you earn or achieve.
However sweet the laid-up stores.
However convenient the dwelling,
You shall not remain there.
However sheltered the port, and however calm the waters,
You shall not anchor there.
However welcome the hospitality that welcomes you,
You are permitted to receive it but a little while.
Afoot and lighthearted, take to the open road,
Healthy, free, the world before you,
The long brown path before you leading wherever you choose.

Say only to one another:
Camerado, I give you my hand!
I give you my love more precious than money,
I give you myself before preaching or law:
Will you give me yourself? Will you come travel with me?
Shall we stick by each other as long as we live?

LOVE IT   LIKE IT

From *Letters to a Young Poet*

—Rainer Maria Rilke, twentieth century
Translated by M. D. Herter Norton

It is . . . good to love: because love is difficult. For one human being to
love another human being: that is perhaps the most difficult task that
has been entrusted to us, the ultimate task, the final test and proof,
the work for which all other work is merely preparation. . . . Loving
does not at first mean merging, surrendering, and uniting with another
person . . . it is a high inducement for the individual to ripen, to become
something in himself, to become world, to become world in himself
for the sake of another person; it is a great, demanding claim on him,
something that chooses him and calls him to vast distances.

"There Is Nothing False in Thee"

—Kenneth Patchen, twentieth century

There is nothing false in thee.
In thy heat the youngest body
Has warmth and light.
In thee the quills of the sun
Find adornment.

What does not die
Is with thee.

Thou art clothed in robes of music.
Thy voice awakens wings.

And still more with thee
Are the flowers of earth made bright.

Upon thy deeps the fiery sails
Of heaven glide.

Thou art the radiance and the joy.
Thy heart shall only fail
When all else has fallen.

What does not perish
Lives in thee.

From *The Little Prince*

—Antoine de Saint-Exupéry, twentieth century
Translated by Richard Howard

"One only understands the things that one tames," said the fox. . . . So the little prince tamed the fox . . . [*and the fox said*], "And now here is my secret, a very simple secret: It is only with the heart that one can see rightly; what is essential is invisible to the eye."

"What is essential is invisible to the eye," the little prince repeated, so that he would be sure to remember.

"It is the time you have wasted for your rose that makes your rose so important."

"It is the time I have wasted for my rose—" said the little prince, so that he would be sure to remember.

"Men have forgotten this truth," said the fox. "But you must not forget it. You become responsible, forever, for what you have tamed. You are responsible for your rose . . ."

"I am responsible for my rose," the little prince repeated, so that he would be sure to remember.

LOVE IT   LIKE IT

From *Broken Arrow,* a 1950 Film

This passage is often mistakenly called an Apache love song.
—Screenplay by Albert Maltz, based on the novel by Elliott Arnold, twentieth century

Now you will feel no rain,
for each of you will be shelter to the other.

tomes of love

The following books may help spark more ideas for your readings:

- *African-American Wedding Readings*, edited by Tamara Nikuradse (Plume, 1999)
- *Into the Garden: A Wedding Anthology*, edited by Robert Hass and Stephen Mitchell (HarperPerennial Library, 1994)
- *Love Letters of Great Men*, vol. 1 (Tribeca Books, 2010)
- *Love Quotes: 300 Sayings and Poems*, compiled by Leonard Roy Frank (Gramercy, 2005)
- *Love Songs and Sonnets* (Everyman's Library Pocket Poets), edited by Peter Washington (Knopf Doubleday, 1997)
- *98 Love Letters That Will Bring You to Your Knees: Poems and Love Letters of Great Men and Women*, edited by John Bradshaw (Madrona Books, 2009)
- *The 100 Best Love Poems of All Time*, edited by Leslie Pockell (Grand Central Publishing, 2004)

- *101 Classic Love Poems*, compiled by Sara L. Whittier (McGraw-Hill, 2003)
- *Proposing on the Brooklyn Bridge: Poems About Marriage*, edited by Ginny Lowe Connors (Poetworks/Grayson Books, 2003)
- *Risking Everything: 110 Poems of Love and Revelation*, edited by Roger Housden (Harmony, 2003)
- *We Grow Old: 53 Chinese Love Poems*, compiled by Yu-Han Chao (Backwaters Press, 2008)
- *Word Lover's Book of Unfamiliar Quotations* by Wesley D. Camp (Prentice Hall, 1999)
- *The World Treasury of Love Stories*, edited by Lucy Rosenthal (Oxford University Press, 1995)
- *You Drive Me Crazy: Love Poems for Real Life*, compiled by Mary D. Esselman and Elizabeth Ash Vélez (Grand Central Publishing, 2005)

Now you will feel no cold,
for each of you will be warmth to the other.

Now there is no loneliness for you;
now there is no more loneliness.

Now you are two bodies,
but there is only one life before you.

Go now to your dwelling place,
and enter into your days together.

And may your days be good
and long upon the earth.

"The Old Song and Dance"
—Kenneth Rexroth, twentieth century

You, because you love me, hold
Fast to me, caress me, be
Quiet and kind, comfort me
With stillness, say nothing at all.
You, because I love you, I
Am strong for you, I uphold
You. The water is alive
Around us. Living water
Runs in the cut earth between
Us. You, my bride, your voice speaks
Over the water to me.
Your hands, your solemn arms,
Cross the water and hold me.
Your body is beautiful.
It speaks across the water.
Bride, sweeter than honey, glad
Of heart, our hearts beat across
The bridge of our arms. Our speech
Is speech of the joy in the night
Of gladness. Our words live.
Our words are children dancing
Forth from us like stars on water.
My bride, my well beloved,
Sweeter than honey, than ripe fruit,

Solemn, grave, a flying bird,
Hold me. Be quiet and kind.
I love you. Be good to me.
I am strong for you. I uphold
You. The dawn of ten thousand
Dawns is afire in the sky.
The water flows in the earth.
The children laugh in the air.

"The Master Speed"

—Robert Frost, twentieth century

No speed of wind or water rushing by
But you have speed far greater. You can climb
Back up a stream of radiance to the sky,
And back through history up the stream of time.
And you were given this swiftness, not for haste
Nor chiefly that you may go where you will,
But in the rush of everything to waste,
That you may have the power of standing still—
Off any still or moving things you say.
Two such as you with such a master speed
Cannot be parted nor be swept away
From one another once you are agreed
That life is only life forevermore
Together wing to wing and oar to oar.

"Tin Wedding Whistle"

LOVE IT   LIKE IT

—Ogden Nash, twentieth century

Though you know it anyhow
Listen to me, darling, now,

Proving what I need not prove
How I know I love you, love.

Near and far, near and far,
I am happy where you are;

Likewise I have never learnt
How to be it where you aren't.

Far and wide, far and wide,
I can walk with you beside;

Furthermore, I tell you what,
I sit and sulk where you are not.

Visitors remark my frown
When you're upstairs and I am down,

Yes, and I'm afraid I pout
When I'm indoors and you are out;

But how contentedly I view
Any room containing you.

In fact I care not where you be,
Just as long as it's with me.

In all your absences I glimpse
Fire and flood and trolls and imps.

Is your train a minute slothful?
I goad the stationmaster wrothful.

When with friends to bridge you drive
I never know if you're alive,

And when you linger late in shops
I long to telephone the cops.

Yet how worth the waiting for,
To see you coming through the door.

Somehow, I can be complacent
Never but with you adjacent.

Near and far, near and far,
I am happy where you are;

Likewise, I have never learnt
How to be it where you aren't.

Then grudge me not my fond endeavor,
To hold you in my sight forever;

Let none, not even you, disparage
Such valid reason for a marriage.

"Invitation to Love"

—Paul Laurence Dunbar, twentieth century

Come when the nights are bright with stars
Or when the moon is mellow;
Come when the sun his golden bars
Drops on the hay-field yellow.
Come in the twilight soft and gray,
Come in the night or come in the day,
Come, O love, whene'er you may,
And you are welcome, welcome.

You are sweet, O Love, dear Love,
You are soft as the nesting dove.
Come to my heart and bring it rest
As the bird flies home to its welcome nest.
Come when my heart is full of grief
Or when my heart is merry;
Come with the falling of the leaf
Or with the redd'ning cherry.
Come when the year's first blossom blows,
Come when the summer gleams and glows,
Come with the winter's drifting snows,
And you are welcome, welcome.

"And I Have You"

—Nikki Giovanni, twentieth century

Rain has drops   Sun has shine
Moon has beams   That make you mine

Rivers have banks   Sands for shores
Hearts have heartbeats   That make me yours

Needles have eyes   Though pins may prick
Elmer has glue   To make things stick

Winter has Spring   Stockings feet
Pepper has mint   To make it sweet

Teachers have lessons   Soup du jour
Lawyers sue bad folks   Doctors cure

All and all this much is true
You have me   And I have you

"You Came, Too"
—Nikki Giovanni, twentieth century

I came to the crowd seeking friends
I came to the crowd seeking love
I came to the crowd for understanding

I found you

I came to the crowd to weep
I came to the crowd to laugh

You dried my tears
You shared my happiness

I went from the crowd seeking you
I went from the crowd seeking me
I went from the crowd forever

You came, too

"somewhere i have never travelled, gladly beyond"
—E. E. Cummings, twentieth century

somewhere i have never travelled,gladly beyond
any experience, your eyes have their silence:
in your most frail gesture are things which enclose me,
or which i cannot touch because they are too near

your slightest look easily will unclose me
though I have closed myself as fingers,
you open always petal by petal myself as Spring opens
(touching skilfully,mysteriously)her first rose

or if your wish be to close me,i and
my life will shut very beautifully,suddenly,
as when the heart of this flower imagines
the snow carefully everywhere descending;

nothing which we are to perceive in this world equals
the power of your intense fragility:whose texture
compels me with the colour of its countries,
rendering death and forever with each breathing

(i do not know what it is about you that closes
and opens;only something in me understands
the voice of your eyes is deeper than all roses)
nobody,not even the rain,has such small hands

LOVE IT LIKE IT

Sonnet XVII

—Pablo Neruda, twentieth century

I do not love you as if you were salt-rose, or topaz,
or the arrow of carnations the fire shoots off.
I love you as certain dark things are to be loved,
in secret, between the shadow and the soul.

I love you as the plant that never blooms
but carries in itself the light of hidden flowers;
thanks to your love a certain solid fragrance,
risen from the earth, lives darkly in my body.

I love you without knowing how, or when, or from where.
I love you straightforwardly, without complexities or pride;
so I love you because I know no other way

than this: where I does not exist, nor you,
so close that your hand on my chest is my hand,
so close that your eyes close as I fall asleep.

LOVE IT LIKE IT

From *Journey to Love*

—William Carlos Williams, twentieth century

It was the love of love,
the love that swallows up all else,
a grateful love,

a love of nature, of people,
of animals,
a love engendering
gentleness and goodness
that moved me
and that I saw in you.

From *Still Life with Woodpecker*
—*Tom Robbins, twentieth century*

LOVE IT   LIKE IT

Love is the ultimate outlaw. It just won't adhere to any rules. The most
any of us can do is to sign on as its accomplice. Instead of vowing to honor
and obey, maybe we should swear to aid and abet. That would mean that
security is out of the question. The words "make" and "stay" become
inappropriate. My love for you has no strings attached. I love you for free.

"Love"
—*Roy Croft, twentieth century*

LOVE IT   LIKE IT

I love you
Not only for what you are,
But for what I am
When I am with you.

I love you,
Not only for what
You have made of yourself,
But for what
You are making of me.

I love you
For the part of me
That you bring out;

I love you
For putting your hand
Into my heaped-up heart
And passing over

All the foolish, weak things
That you can't help
Dimly seeing there,

> ### too much for words?
>
> If you come across a
> reading that you love
> that's too long to use,
> feel free to edit it to the
> right length. Just make
> sure you make a note
> that the poem or
> passage has been
> trimmed! Alternatively, a
> long piece can be divided
> between two readers.

And for drawing out
Into the light
All the beautiful belongings
That no one else had looked
Quite far enough to find

I love you because you
Are helping me to make
Of the lumber of my life
Not a tavern
But a temple.

Out of the works
Of my every day
Not a reproach
But a song.

I love you
Because you have done
More than any creed
Could have done
To make me good.
And more than any fate
Could have done
To make me happy.

You have done it
Without a touch,
Without a word,
Without a sign.
You have done it

By being yourself.
Perhaps that is what
Being a friend means,
After all.

"Happily Married"

—Deborah Garrison, twentieth century

Almost home
on the longest day of the year,
I saw two birds on a telephone wire:
two beaks, two sharp-peaked ruffs,
two tails that stuck down stiff
like two closed fans
all matched up neatly,
and against the faintly
yellow pre-dusk sky
the birds and wire
were all one color,
a fading black
or darkening gray.

Sometimes the smallest thing
brings harmony in
through the eye.
Or was it that I
on that particular day
had harmony to bring
to what I saw?
That I'd even looked up
seemed a piece of marital
good luck, and that they didn't
move as I passed by—

I wondered how long in fact
they'd sit that way.

Lyrics to "Dance Me to the End of Love"

—Leonard Cohen, twentieth century

Dance me to your beauty with a burning violin
Dance me through the panic 'til I'm gathered safely in
And dance me to the end of love

Let me see your beauty when the witnesses are gone
Let me feel you moving like they do in Babylon
Show me slowly what I only know the limits of
And dance me to the end of love

Dance me to the wedding now, dance me on and on
Dance me very tenderly and dance me very long
We're both of us beneath our love, we're both of us above
And dance me to the end of love

Dance me to the children who are asking to be born
Dance me through the curtains that our kisses have outworn
Raise a tent of shelter now, though every thread is torn
And dance me to the end of love

Dance me to your beauty with a burning violin
Dance me through the panic till I'm gathered safely in
Touch me with your naked hand or touch me with your glove
Dance me to the end of love

Lyrics to "To Make You Feel My Love"

—*Bob Dylan, twentieth century*

When the rain is blowing in your face
And the whole world is on your case
I could offer you a warm embrace
To make you feel my love

When the evening shadows and the stars appear
And there is no one there to dry your tears
I could hold you for a million years
To make you feel my love

I know you haven't made your mind up yet
But I would never do you wrong
I've known it from the moment that we met
No doubt in my mind where you belong

I'd go hungry, I'd go black and blue
I'd go crawling down the avenue
There's nothing that I wouldn't do
To make you feel my love

The storms are raging on the rollin' sea
And on the highway of regret
The winds of change are blowing wild and free
You ain't seen nothing like me yet

I could make you happy, make your dreams come true
Nothing that I wouldn't do
Go to the ends of the earth for you
To make you feel my love

"Falling"

—Rob Hardy, twentieth century

You already know about love.
You fall in love. Falling is easy. Maybe you don't
see it coming. Maybe you brace yourself against the wind in the door,
see the earth circling below
and jump. Falling is easy. It feels like flight.
You feel your kinship with clouds, with light,
stuff of stars, atoms that float and fall,
meteors, stars that still glow
with the start of everything.
You raise your arms like wings. Butterfly
or belly-flop. You feel the earth expanding—
don't look down. Reach for the cord.
Falling is easy. But is this love
or gravity? Pull the cord. Yes—
love blossoms from the weight you carry,
the question, the tug at your heart.
The parachute pops like a cork.
Now you float in the arms of the atmosphere,
milkweed floss, dandelion seed,
no longer afraid to take root in the earth—
but still floating a while, ecstasy and trust, your high-
altitude heart settling back into a steadier beat,
the tilt of the earth, seasons and days.
But here you are floating—buoyed by invitations
and arrangements. Now you look down.
The ground looms like a date, circled for landing.
The fields looks like RSVPs. Your feet touch. The parachute
falls around you like a wedding dress.
You've landed together. Dance while the earth steadies
beneath your feet. Hold each other up.
Now you will walk together into ordinary days.
Your parachute may become a maternity dress, a mortgage,
a tissue for your tears. It may be divided into diapers,

waterproof sheets, a layette, stories to tell your grandchildren.
Days may come when you forget how it felt to float.
But still this moment of landing lives inside you,
when the touch of the ground felt like a vow—
I will always be there. I will catch you if you fall.

"The Invitation"

—Oriah, twentieth century

It doesn't interest me
what you do for a living.
I want to know
what you ache for
and if you dare to dream
of meeting your heart's longing.

It doesn't interest me
how old you are.
I want to know
if you will risk
looking like a fool
for love
for your dream
for the adventure of being alive.

It doesn't interest me
what planets are
squaring your moon . . .
I want to know
if you have touched
the centre of your own sorrow
if you have been opened
by life's betrayals
or have become shrivelled and closed
from fear of further pain.

I want to know
if you can sit with pain
mine or your own
without moving to hide it
or fade it
or fix it.

love letters as readings

The author of the perfect ceremony reading might be you. Check to see if you have any saved love letters, e-mails, or texts from your relationship. They might make for ultrapersonalized readings or quotes to include in your ceremony.

I want to know
if you can be with joy
mine or your own
if you can dance with wildness
and let the ecstasy fill you
to the tips of your fingers and toes
without cautioning us
to be careful
to be realistic
to remember the limitations
of being human.

It doesn't interest me
if the story you are telling me
is true.
I want to know if you can
disappoint another
to be true to yourself.
If you can bear
the accusation of betrayal
and not betray your own soul.
If you can be faithless
and therefore trustworthy.

I want to know if you can see Beauty
even when it is not pretty
every day.
And if you can source your own life
from its presence.

I want to know
if you can live with failure
yours and mine
and still stand at the edge of the lake
and shout to the silver of the full moon,
"Yes."

It doesn't interest me
to know where you live
or how much money you have.
I want to know if you can get up
after the night of grief and despair

weary and bruised to the bone
and do what needs to be done
to feed the children.

It doesn't interest me
who you know
or how you came to be here.
I want to know if you will stand
in the centre of the fire
with me
and not shrink back.

It doesn't interest me
where or what or with whom
you have studied.
I want to know
what sustains you
from the inside
when all else falls away.

I want to know
if you can be alone
with yourself
and if you truly like
the company you keep
in the empty moments.

☐   ☐
LOVE IT   LIKE IT

From *Love*

—Leo Buscaglia, twentieth century

In discussing love, it would be well to consider the following premises:
One cannot give what he does not possess. To give love you must possess
     love.
One cannot teach what he does not understand. To teach love you must
     comprehend love.
One cannot know what he does not study. To study love you must live in
     love.
One cannot appreciate what he does not recognize. To recognize love
     you must be receptive to love.
One cannot have doubt about that which he wishes to trust. To trust love
     you must be convinced of love.

One cannot admit what he does not yield to. To yield to love you must be
   vulnerable to love.
One cannot live what he does not dedicate himself to. To dedicate
   yourself to love you must be forever growing in love.

From *The Prophet*
—*Kahlil Gibran, twentieth century*

LOVE IT   LIKE IT

Love one another, but make not a bond of love;
Let it rather be a moving sea between the shores of your souls.
Fill each other's cup but drink not from one cup.
Give one another of your bread but eat not from the same loaf.
Sing and dance together and be joyous, but let each one of you be alone,
Even as the strings of a lute are alone though they quiver with the same
   music.

Give your hearts, but not into each other's keeping.
For only the hand of Life can contain your hearts.
And stand together yet not too near together:
For the pillars of the temple stand apart,
And the oak tree and the cypress grow not in each other's shadow.

"Two Trees"
—*Janet Miles, twentieth century*

LOVE IT   LIKE IT

A portion of your soul has been
entwined with mine.
A gentle kind of togetherness, while
separately we stand.
As two trees deeply rooted in
separate plots of ground,
While their topmost branches
come together,
Forming a miracle of lace
against the heavens.

LOVE IT   LIKE IT

"The Sonnet"

—Arthur Davison Ficke, twentieth century

Love is the simplest of all earthly things.
It needs no grandeur of celestial trust
In more than what it is, no holy wings:
It stands with honest feet in honest dust.
And is the body's blossoming in clear air
Of trustfulness and joyance when alone
Two mortals pass beyond the hour's despair
And claim that Paradise which is their own.
Amid a universe of sweat and blood,
Beyond the glooms of all the nations' hate,
Lovers, forgetful of the poisoned mood
Of the loud world, in secret ere too late
A gentle sacrament may celebrate
Before their private altar of the good.

LOVE IT   LIKE IT

"Barter"

—Sara Teasdale, twentieth century

Life has loveliness to sell,
All beautiful and splendid things,
Blue waves whitened on a cliff,
Soaring fire that sways and sings,
And children's faces looking up,
Holding wonder like a cup.
Life has loveliness to sell
Music like a curve of gold,
Scent of pine trees in the rain,
Eyes that love you, arms that hold,
And for your spirit's still delight,
Holy thoughts that star the night.
Spend all you have for loveliness,
Buy it and never count the cost;
For one white singing hour of peace
Count many a year of strife well lost,
And for a breath of ecstacy
Give all you have been, or could be.

"We Become New"

—Marge Piercy, twentieth century

How it feels to be touching
you: an Io moth, orange
and yellow as pollen,
wings through the night
miles to mate,
could crumble in the hand.

Yet our meaning together
is hardy as an onion
and layered.
Goes into the blood like garlic.
Sour as rose hips,
gritty as whole grain,

fragrant as thyme honey.
When I am turning slowly
in the woven hammocks of our talk,
when I am chocolate melting into you,
I taste everything new
in your mouth.

You are not my old friend.
How did I used to sit
and look at you? Now
though I seem to be standing still
I am flying flying flying
in the trees of your eyes.

"Unclench Yourself"

—Marge Piercy, twentieth century

Open, love, open.
I tell you we are able
I tell you we are able
now and then gently
with hands and feet
cold even as fish
to curl into a tangle
and grow a single hide,

slowly to unknit all other skin
and rest in flesh
and rest in flesh entire.
Come all the way in, love,
it is a river
with a strong current
but its brown waters
will not drown you.
Let go.
Do not hold out
your head.
The current knows the bottom
better than your feet can.
You will find
that in this river
we can breathe
we can breathe
and under water see
small gardens and bright fish
too tender
too tender
for the air.

"Scaffolding"

—Seamus Heaney, twentieth century

Masons, when they start upon a building,
Are careful to test out the scaffolding;

Make sure that planks won't slip at busy points,
Secure all ladders, tighten bolted joints.

And yet all this comes down when the job's done
Showing off walls of sure and solid stone.

So if, my dear, there sometimes seem to be
Old bridges breaking between you and me

Never fear. We may let the scaffolds fall
Confident that we have built our wall.

"I Sat in the Happiness"

—Yehuda Amichai, twentieth century

Your eyes withstood great cold
And great heat
Like beautiful glass
And remained clear.

I sat in the happiness. Like straps
Of a heavy knapsack,
Love cut the shoulders of my heart.

Your eyes forced on me
A history of new life.

I sat in the happiness. From now on
I will be just one side in the dictionary,
Expressed or explained.

Your eyes count and count.

LOVE IT   LIKE IT

"Litany"

—Billy Collins, twenty-first century

You are the bread and the knife,
the crystal goblet and the wine.
You are the dew on the morning grass
and the burning wheel of the sun.
You are the white apron of the baker
and the marsh birds suddenly in flight.

However, you are not the wind in the orchard,
the plums on the counter,
or the house of cards.
And you are certainly not the pine-scented air.
There is just no way you are the pine-scented air.

It is possible that you are the fish under the bridge,
maybe even the pigeon on the general's head,
but you are not even close
to being the field of cornflowers at dusk.

LOVE IT   LIKE IT

And a quick look in the mirror will show
that you are neither the boots in the corner
nor the boat asleep in its boathouse.

It might interest you to know,
speaking of the plentiful imagery of the world,
that I am the sound of rain on the roof.

I also happen to be the shooting star,
the evening paper blowing down an alley,
and the basket of chestnuts on the kitchen table.

I am also the moon in the trees
and the blind woman's tea cup.
But don't worry, I am not the bread and the knife.
You are still the bread and the knife.
You will always be the bread and the knife,
not to mention the crystal goblet and—somehow—
the wine.

"Loving the Wrong Person"

—Andrew Boyd, twenty-first century

We're all seeking that special person who is right for us.
But if you've been through enough relationships, you begin to suspect
    there's no right person, just different flavors of wrong.
Why is this?
Because you yourself are wrong in some way, and you seek out partners
    who are wrong in some complementary way.
But it takes a lot of living to grow fully into your own wrongness.
It isn't until you finally run up against your deepest demons, your
    unsolvable problems—the ones that make you truly who you are—that
    you're ready to find a life-long mate.
Only then do you finally know what you're looking for. You're looking for
    the wrong person.
But not just any wrong person: the right wrong person—someone you
    lovingly gaze upon and think,
"This is the problem I want to have."

LOVE IT   LIKE IT

"Begin"

—Brendan Kennelly, twenty-first century

Begin again to the summoning birds
to the sight of light at the window,
begin to the roar of morning traffic
all along Pembroke Road.

Every beginning is a promise
born in light and dying in dark
determination
and exaltation of springtime
flowering the way to work.
Begin to the pageant of queuing girls
the arrogant loneliness of swans in the canal
bridges linking the past and the future
old friends passing through with us still.
Begin to the loneliness that cannot end
since it perhaps is what makes us
begin,
begin to wonder
at unknown faces
at crying birds in the sudden rain
at branches stark in the willing sunlight
at seagulls foraging for bread
at couples sharing a sunny secret
alone together while making good.
Though we live in a world
that dreams of ending
that always seems about to give in
something that will not acknowledge conclusion
insists that we forever begin.

☐ LOVE IT ☐ LIKE IT

"A Blessing for Wedding"
—Jane Hirshfield, twenty-first century

Today when persimmons ripen
Today when fox-kits come out of their den into snow
Today when the spotted egg releases its wren song
Today when the maple sets down its red leaves
Today when windows keep their promise to open
Today when fire keeps its promise to warm
Today when someone you love has died
   or someone you never met has died
Today when someone you love has been born
   or someone you will not meet has been born
Today when rain leaps to the waiting of roots in their dryness
Today when starlight bends to the roofs of the hungry and tired
Today when someone sits long inside his last sorrow
Today when someone steps into the heat of her first embrace
Today, let this light bless you
With these friends let it bless you
With snow-scent and lavender bless you
Let the vow of this day keep itself wildly and wholly
Spoken and silent, surprise you inside your ears
Sleeping and waking, unfold itself inside your eyes
Let its fierceness and tenderness hold you
Let its vastness be undisguised in all your days

☐ LOVE IT ☐ LIKE IT

"Rings"
—Carol Ann Duffy, twenty-first century

I might have raised your hand to the sky
to give you the ring surrounding the moon
or looked to twin the rings of your eyes
with mine
or added a ring to the rings of a tree
by forming a handheld circle with you, thee,
or walked with you
where a ring of church-bells,
looped the fields,
or kissed a lipstick ring on your cheek,
a pressed flower,
or met with you
in the ring of an hour,

and another hour . . .
I might
have opened your palm to the weather, turned, turned,
till your fingers were ringed in rain
or held you close,
they were playing our song,
in the ring of a slow dance
or carved our names
in the rough ring of a heart
or heard the ring of an owl's hoot
as we headed home in the dark

or the ring, first thing,
of chorussing birds
waking the house
or given the ring of a boat, rowing the lake,
or the ring of swans, monogamous, two,
or the watery rings made by the fish
as they leaped and splashed
or the ring of the sun's reflection there . . .
I might have tied
a blade of grass,
a green ring for your finger,
or told you the ring of a sonnet by heart
or brought you a lichen ring,
found on a warm wall,
or given a ring of ice in winter
or in the snow
sung with you the five gold rings of a carol
or stolen a ring of your hair
or whispered the word in your ear
that brought us here,
where nothing and no one is wrong,
and therefore I give you this ring.

Notes

rings and other rituals

The wedding rituals of a culture or country, an ethnic or religious group, or even a family serve much the same purpose—they are tried-and-true symbols of the joining of two people in marriage. They are the ways the community—the people present at your wedding, but also everyone else who follows the same traditions and shares the same beliefs—recognizes the step the two of you are taking, and a way for you to take your place next to all the couples who came before you. They are also a way to include the people close to you in your ceremony.

EXCHANGING RINGS

After you exchange vows, you will exchange wedding rings. Your officiant may say a few words first about their symbolism; if you're having a religious ceremony, your priest, minister, or rabbi will likely say a blessing over them, as well. Below are some phrases you can use during the exchange, or you may choose to compose your own. The most simple and traditional phrase: "With this ring, I thee wed."

protestant/presbyterian

"In token and pledge of our constant faith and abiding love, with this ring I thee wed, in the name of the Father, and of the Son, and of the Holy Spirit. Amen."

lutheran

"I give you this ring as a sign of my love and faithfulness.
Receive this ring as a token of wedded love and faith."

episcopal

"I give you this ring as a symbol of my vow, and with all that I am, and all that I have, I honor you, in the name of the Father, and of the Son, and of the Holy Spirit [or: in the name of God]."

methodist

"I give you this ring as a sign of my vow, and with all that I am, and all that I have, I honor you [in the name of the Father, and of the Son, and of the Holy Spirit]."

"In token and pledge of the vow between us made, with this ring I thee wed; in the name of the Father, and of the Son, and of the Holy Spirit. Amen."

baptist

"With this ring I thee wed, and all my worldly goods I thee endow. In sickness and in health, in poverty or in wealth, till death do us part."

catholic

"Take this ring as a sign of my love and fidelity. In the name of the Father, and of the Son, and of the Holy Spirit."

"In the name of the Father, and of the Son, and of the Holy Spirit. Take and wear this ring as a pledge of my fidelity."

unitarian

"With this ring, I wed you and pledge you my love now and forever."

jewish

"*Haray at mekudeshet lee beh-taba'at zo keh-dat Moshe veh-Yisrael*: Behold, you are consecrated to me with this ring according to the laws of Moses and Israel."

"Thou are consecrated unto me with this ring as my wife/husband, according to the laws of Moses and Israel."

"Be sanctified to me with this ring, in accordance with the laws of Moses and Israel."

nondenominational

"With this ring, I thee wed, as a symbol of love that has neither beginning nor end."

"I give you this ring; wear it with love and joy."

"As this ring encircles your finger from this day forward, year in and year out, so will my love forever encircle you."

"This ring I give you as a sign of our constant faith and abiding love."

"I give you this ring as a reminder that I love you every day of your life."

"This ring I give you in token of my devotion and love, and with my heart I pledge to you all that I am. With this ring I marry you and join my life to yours."

"I offer you this ring as a symbol of my enduring love. I ask that you take it and wear it so that all may know you are touched by my love."

"Go little ring to that same sweet
That hath my heart in her domain . . ."
—*Geoffrey Chaucer*

updating your ring exchange

There are a few special twists that you can add to personalize your ring exchange. You can wear each other's rings up until the exchange, kiss each other's ring fingers before putting them on, or include your guests by having a "ring passing." This ritual involves sending both wedding rings through all the guests prior to exchanging them, as a demonstration of their support of the couple.

"This ring is round and hath no end,
So is my love unto my friend."
—*Sixteenth-century vow*

"I give you this ring. Wear it with love and joy. As this ring has no end, neither shall my love for you. I choose you to be my wife/husband this day and every day."
—*Bill Swetmon, ordained nondenominational minister*

"With this ring, I give you my promise that from this day forward you shall never walk alone. My heart will be your shelter, my arms will be your home. We will walk together through life as partners and best friends. I promise that I shall always do my best to love and accept you exactly the way you are. With this ring, I give you your freedom and my trust in you. I give you my heart until the end of time; I have no greater gift to give."
—*Adapted from* Illuminata: Thoughts, Prayers, Rites of Passage, *by Marianne Williamson*

native american

"Love freely given has no beginning and no end, no one giver and no one receiver, for each is a giver and a receiver. May these rings always remind you of the vows you have made."

safekeeping your rings

Having a ring bearer is a great way to include a young family member— or the family dog—in your wedding ceremony. Just make sure the real wedding rings are with the best man, or another attendant, and tie fake rings to the ring pillow for the tyke or pup to carry.

MORE EXCHANGES

Almost all weddings, regardless of culture or religion, contain a ritual of exchange. The bride and groom may exchange flowers and food as a symbolic gesture, or they may exchange tangible objects, such as rings and money.

triple ring exchange (eastern orthodox)

The wedding rings are blessed during the betrothal ceremony. After reciting blessings and biblical passages, the priest makes the sign of the cross while holding the rings and declaring the betrothal. He may hold the rings in his hands while pressing the foreheads of the couple three times each. Then, either the priest or the *koumbaros* (the best man) exchanges the rings between the couple's fingers three times, signifying that the weakness of one will be compensated by the other.

words of engravement

Here are some ideas for words of love engraved inside your wedding rings:

I love you

Our love is eternal

To my soul mate

C.R. to D.L. Jul.10

Always

Forever

Eternity

C & D forever (use your first initials)

I thee wed

All my love

I marry you

You have my heart

My heart is in your hands

Never to part

To my wife/husband

Soul mates forever

I'm always with you

To have and to hold

Schmoopie (your private nicknames for each other)

Here is my heart, guard it well!

No one but you

God for Me Provided Thee

God Unite Both in Love

In Thy Brest My Hart Doth Rest (Old English)

Por tous jours ("For all days" —fifteenth-century French)

Joie sans fin ("Joy without end" —French)

Mon coeur est à vous ("You have my heart" —French)

Je t'aime ("I love you" —French)

Mon amour ("My love" —French)

En bien aimer ("To encircle with love" — fifteenth-century French)

Il mio cuore e il tuo per sempre ("My heart is yours forever" —Italian)

Amore mio ("My love" —Italian)

Vivo per lei ("I live for her" —Italian)

Myn Genyst ("My heart" —Old German)

Mizpah ("God, watch between us when we are absent from one another" —Hebrew, Genesis 31:48–49)

Ani L'dodi V'dodi Li ("I am my beloved's and my beloved is mine" —Hebrew, Song of Solomon 2:16)

Semper amemus ("Let us always love" —Latin)

Semper fidelis ("Always faithful" —Latin)

Pari passu ("With equal step" —Latin)

Amor vincit omnia ("Love conquers all" —Latin)

Deus nos iunxit ("God joined us" —Latin)

百年好合 ("Happily ever after" —Chinese)

花好月圆 (" Blissful harmony" —Chinese)

Because the right hand has a rich and symbolic history in the Eastern Orthodox Church, the rings are usually placed on the third finger of the right hand.

crowning ceremony (eastern orthodox)

The crowning is the centerpiece of an Eastern Orthodox wedding ceremony. Garland wreaths are often fashioned into ornate crowns as a symbol of glory and honor. Crowns can also be made of orange blossoms, myrtle leaves, or semiprecious stones and metals. Threads of gold and crimson are sometimes used to represent the royalty of marriage. The *koumbaros* presents the couple with two crowns joined by a white ribbon, symbolizing their union. The priest then places the crowns on the couple's heads while they face the altar. The *koumbaros* swaps the crowns on the couple's heads three times, symbolizing the Holy Trinity. According to ancient custom, the crowns are to stay with the couple for life—some couples are even buried in them.

garland exchange (hindu and hawaiian)

In both Hindu and Hawaiian ceremonies, the bride and groom exchange garlands of flowers. In Hindu weddings, the bride and groom meet in front of the *mandap* (wedding platform), where they exchange gifts of flower garlands before stepping onto the platform in a ceremony called Kanya Baran Jaimala. They then wear the garlands around their necks throughout the ceremony. Hawaiian couples exchange leis (the jewels of the ancient Hawaiians) and seal their union by rubbing noses.

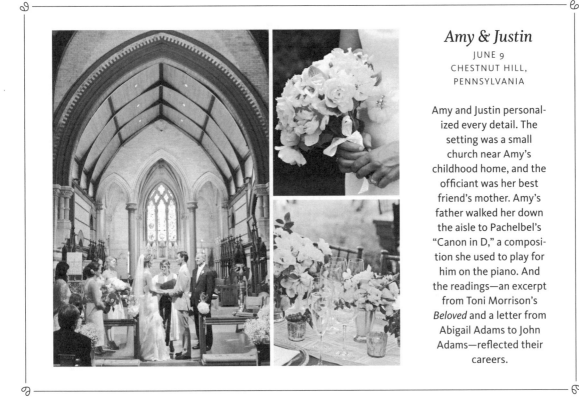

Amy & Justin
JUNE 9
CHESTNUT HILL,
PENNSYLVANIA

Amy and Justin personalized every detail. The setting was a small church near Amy's childhood home, and the officiant was her best friend's mother. Amy's father walked her down the aisle to Pachelbel's "Canon in D," a composition she used to play for him on the piano. And the readings—an excerpt from Toni Morrison's *Beloved* and a letter from Abigail Adams to John Adams—reflected their careers.

kola nuts (nigeria)

In Africa, kola nuts represent healing; giving them to each other (often after the vows) is a symbol of the couple's commitment to work out their differences and support each other through hard times.

arras (spanish and latino)

During Catholic ceremonies in Spain, Panama, and Mexico, the groom presents the bride with thirteen gold coins, known as *arras*, to represent his ability to support her. The coins are blessed by the priest and passed through the hands of the newlyweds several times, ending with the bride. Want to make the ritual a little more balanced? Consider giving each other coins, to symbolize shared responsibility.

meher (muslim)

Included in the marriage contract is a *meher*, a formal statement specifying the monetary amount the groom will present to the bride. It is traditionally considered the bride's security and guarantee of freedom within the marriage. There are two parts to the *meher*: a "prompt," due before the marriage is consummated, and a deferred amount, given to the bride throughout her life. Today, many couples use the ring as the prompt, since the groom presents it during the ceremony; the deferred amount can be a small sum offered as a formality, or it can actually be a gift of money, land, jewelry, or even an education. The gift remains the bride's to use as she pleases.

rose ceremony (nondenominational)

This modern ritual incorporates one of the most beloved symbols of romantic love—the rose. A white one is used in honor of the wedding day.

> Groom (handing bride the rose): "_____, take this rose as a symbol of my love. It began as a bud and blossomed, just as my love for you has grown and blossomed."

> Bride (placing rose into a bud vase filled with water): "I take this rose, a symbol of your love, and I place it into water, a symbol of life. For, just as this rose cannot survive without water, I cannot survive without you."

Groom: "In remembrance of this day, I will give you a white rose each year on our anniversary, as a reaffirmation of my love and the vows spoken here today."

Bride: "And I will refill this vase with water each year, ready to receive your gift, in reaffirmation of my love and the vows spoken here today."

[At this time the couple may join hands around the vase to exchange their vows; or this ritual can be done separately, after the vows have been spoken and rings have been exchanged.]

GIVING THANKS

Wedding ceremonies are largely focused on the bride and groom, but their families are an important part of their marriage, and there are many rituals that recognize the couple's ancestors, their God, and the path that brought them to this day.

libation ceremony (africa)

Libation is a traditional African ceremony in which water is poured on the ground in the four directions that the wind comes from in remembrance and honor of the couple's ancestors, calling on them to be present to witness the marriage. Often a family elder does the honors, and guests respond to the blessing with the word *ase*, meaning "so it may be." Here is a sample libation prayer:

"All praise to God Almighty. Praise to our African ancestors and roots. God gave his power for the roots of the trees to spread its branches wide. If man does not know his roots, then he does not know his God. Let the spirit of God and ancestors bring us closer in unity."

homage to the fire god, agni (hindu)

In Hindu weddings, the following is recited over a ceremonial fire:

"O Lord Fire, First Created Being! Be thou the over-lord and give food and drink to this household. O Lord Fire, who reigns in richness and vitality over all the worlds, come take your proper seat in this home! Accept the offering made here, protect the one who makes

them, be our protector on this day, O you who see into the hearts
of all created beings!"

tea or sake ceremony (china and japan)

In China and Japan, it is part of the wedding ceremony for the couple
to present their parents with tea (in China) or sake (in Japan) to show
respect and to represent the new family bond. In a traditional Chinese
tea ceremony, the bride serves tea with sugar to the groom and his
family, the sweetness representing a wish for sweet relations. Japanese
couples each drink three sips from three sake cups, then offer the rice
drink to both sets of parents.

UNIFYING RITUALS

There are many rituals that demonstrate the couple's commitment to
each other and their new bond as a married couple. In many cultures,
the hands of the bride and groom are literally tied together.

handfasting (afrocentric)

In some African tribes, the bride and groom have their wrists tied
together with cloth or braided grass. To symbolize your own unity, have
your officiant or a close friend tie your wrists together with a piece of
kente cloth or a strand of cowrie shells (symbols of fertility and prosperity) while affirming your oneness.

handfasting (celtic)

Handfasting was practiced by the Celts, among other people, during
the Middle Ages. A year after the couple was handfasted, they were
officially considered a married couple. Many practicing pagans and
Wiccans use the ritual as their wedding ceremony. It involves much
reverence of nature and also the tying together of the bride's and
groom's wrists or hands.

Here are some excerpts from a handfasting rite:

Priestess/officiant: "Welcome, friends, as we gather to celebrate the
marriage of _____ and _____. Divine One, I ask thee to bless this
couple, their love, and their marriage as long as they shall live in
love together. May they each enjoy a healthy life filled with joy, love,
stability, and fertility." [Turns to the east.]

"Blessed be by the element of air. May you be blessed with communication, intellectual growth, and wisdom." [Turns to the south.]

"Blessed be by the element of fire. May you be blessed with harmony, vitality, creativity, and passion." [Turns to the west.]

"Blessed be by the element of water. May you be blessed with friendship, intuition, caring, understanding, and love." [Turns to the north.]

"Blessed be by the element of earth. May you be blessed with tenderness, happiness, compassion, and sensuality. . . .

"Love has its seasons, the same as does the Earth. In the spring of love is the discovery of each other, the pulse of the senses, the getting to know the mind and heart of the other; a blooming like the buds and flowers of springtime.

"In the summer of love comes the strength, the commitment to each other, the most active part of life, perhaps including the giving of life back to itself through children; the sharing of joys and sorrows, the learning to be humans who are each complete and whole but who can merge each with the other, as the trees grow green and tall in the heat of the sun.

"In the fall of love is the contentment of love that knows the other completely. Passion remains, and ease of companionship. The heart smoothes love into a steady light, glorious as the autumn leaves.

"In the winter of love, there is parting, and sorrow. But love remains, as do the stark and bare tree trunks in the snow, ready for the renewal of love in the spring as life and love begin anew.

"Now is the time of summer. _____ and _____ have gathered before their friends to make a statement of their commitment to each other, to their love."

[Couple faces each other.] "Do you now commit to each other to love, honor, respect each other, to communicate with each other, to look to your own emotional health so that you can relate in a healthy way, and provide a healthy home for children if you choose to have them; to be a support and comfort for your partner in times of sickness and health, as long as love shall last?"

Together: "We do."

[After the vows and ring exchange, the couple's hands are bound together in a "love knot." The priestess says something along the lines of: "With this cord, I bind you to the vows that you each have made."]

handfasting (egypt)

Marriages among the fellahin of Northern Egypt take place at night.

The bride and groom, along with family and friends, walk through the streets to the church. As they walk, the men carry lanterns and the women sound the joyful zagharit, a shrill, vibrating call. When they arrive, the priest takes a silk cord and passes it over the groom's right shoulder and under his left arm, tying the thread into a looped knot. The priest says prayers and then unties the groom. He then ties the two wedding rings together with the cord. He questions the bride and groom on their intentions, then unties the rings and places them on the couple's fingers.

hasthagranthi (hindu)

In this ritual the couple's hands are tied together with string. What follows is the Shakhohar, the family roots union, in which the parents place their hands on top of the couple's to express their union as a

Joseph & Lallo
SEPTEMBER 15
SONOMA, CALIFORNIA

The couple wrote their own vows, but neither thought they'd be able to say them in front of a crowd without getting emotional. "We were both so nervous, we ended up shortening the vows to be able to make it through the ceremony," Joseph says. Luckily, one of the couple's friends broke the ice by doing a surprise reading of the lyrics of "Like a Virgin" by Madonna. "It certainly brought laughter and joy into the atmosphere," Joseph says.

family. A long scarf is then wrapped around the couple in a ritual called Gath Bandhan.

circling the table (eastern orthodox)

The priest (and sometimes the *koumbaros*, or best man, too) leads the couple three times around the altar, on which a Bible and cross rest. This ritual predates Christianity—it originated in Judaism—and represents the dance around the Ark of the Covenant. The choir sings three hymns as the couple circles. In this act, they take their first steps as a married couple, with the Church (through the priest) leading them.

circling (jewish)

When the couple first steps underneath the huppah, their wedding canopy, the bride circles the groom seven times, representing the seven wedding blessings and seven days of Creation, and demonstrating that the groom is the center of her world. To make the ancient ritual reciprocal, many couples opt to circle each other.

lazo (latino)

In Guatemala, the couple bind themselves together during the ceremony with a silver rope, or *lazo*. Mexican couples perform a similar ritual, where a rosary or white rope is wound around their shoulders in a figure eight to symbolize their union. While the couple is bound together, the priest may recite the following: "Let the union of binding together this rosary of the Blessed Virgin Mary be an inspiration to you both. Remember the holiness necessary to preserve your new family can only be obtained by mutual sacrifice and love."

SYMBOLIC RITUALS

In some of the most ancient wedding rituals, the couple demonstrates their love and devotion by using symbolic objects, such as candles, food, and even brooms.

seven steps (hindu)

In Hindu weddings, after the couple has taken seven steps around the fire at their ceremony, their bond is sealed, and the following is recited in a ritual, Saptha Padhi. It also makes a beautiful reading on its own.

"We have taken the seven steps. You have become mine forever. Yes, we have become partners. I have become yours. Hereafter I cannot live without you. Do not live without me. Let us share the joys. We are word and meaning, united. You are thought and I am sound.

"May the nights be honey-sweet for us; may the mornings be honey-sweet for us; may the earth be honey-sweet for us; may the heavens be honey-sweet for us.

"May the plants be honey-sweet for us; may the sun be all honey for us; may the cows yield us honey-sweet milk!

"As the heavens are stable, as the earth is stable, as the mountains are stable, as the whole universe is stable, so may our union be permanently settled."

honey ceremony (multifaith)

This ritual revolves around honey, a symbolic food since ancient times and crossing many cultures.

"Honey is a symbol of the sweetness in life. And so, with this dish of honey, we proclaim this day as a day of great joy and celebration—a day to remember—Your Day. We thank you, Allah [or substitute deity name], for creating this divine substance, and ask you to bless it, even as you will bless this holy union. Amen."

[Groom dips his little finger into the honey and touches bride's tongue with it; bride does the same, touching groom's tongue.]

"As together you now share this honey, so may you, under God's guidance, in perfect love and devotion to each other, share your lives together, and thereby may you find life's joys doubly gladdening, its bitterness sweetened, and all things hallowed by time, companionship and love."

unity candle (catholic)

This joining ritual is quite popular at Catholic weddings, but its significance is universal: the joining of the couple as a new family, as well as the merging of their two original families. Usually the officiant will explain the unity candle's meaning—the following is an example:

"_____ and _____ , the two separate candles symbolize your separate lives. I ask that each of you take one of the lit candles and that together you light the center candle.

"The individual candles represent your lives before today. Lighting the center candle represents that your two lives are now joined to one light, and represents the joining together of your two lives and families to one."

After the candle is lit, your officiant or an honored friend or family member may recite a blessing, such as the following:

"May the blessing of light
Be with you always,
Light without and light within.
And may the sun shine
Upon you and warm your heart
Until it glows
Like a great fire
So that others may feel
The warmth of your love
For one another."

candle ceremony (wiccan)

The words of this Wiccan candle ceremony focus on the couple's union in marriage. However, this candle ceremony focuses less on two families uniting (as a unity candle ceremony does) than on two individuals coming together, yet remaining independent. Interfaith or nondenominational couples could certainly include it in their ceremony.

The priestess asks the bride and groom to each light a candle. Another candle stands unlit.

"These two candles are yourselves. Each of you is a whole and complete human being.
   "_____ , speak to us of who you are." [Groom describes himself.]
   "_____ , speak to us of who you are." [Bride describes herself.]
   "Together, light the third candle, but extinguish not the first two. For in marriage you do not lose yourself; you add something new, a relationship, the capacity to merge into one another without losing sight of your individual self. Together, speak to us of who you are as a couple." [Bride and groom alternate speaking.]

candle ceremony (nondenominational)

Here is an example of a nondenomination candle ceremony, done with a central "eternal light" and two individual candles for the bride and groom:

> "Now, we're going to engage in a ceremony of spiritual symbolism. Ancient sages tell us that for each of us, there is a candle, a symbol of our own inner light, but that no one can kindle his or her own candle. Each of us needs someone else to kindle it for us. When two people fall in love, they kindle each other's candles, creating great light and joy and glorious expectations.
>
> "_____ and _____ , I'd like you to remember when it was in your relationship that you first realized you were truly in love and wanted to spend the rest of your lives together. And holding that thought . . .
>
> "_____ , take this candle [groom picks up candle], symbol of the inner light in _____ . Light it by the eternal light, with the dedication to rekindle it again and again, whenever necessary."

And

> "_____ , take this candle [bride picks up candle], symbol of the inner light in _____ . Light it by the eternal light, with the dedication to rekindle it again and again, whenever necessary.
>
> "With these candles, we can see how to achieve a beautiful marriage. In your marriage, you will try to bring these lights, the symbols of yourselves, closer and closer to each other, until they become one [bride and groom join their flames and hold them together]—one great torch of light, a radiant symbol of love, joy, peace, and harmony. This is the mystery of the union of two becoming one.
>
> "Yet, it is vitally important to remember that there are always really two [couple divides their flames] in a marriage, each with his or her own desires, yearnings, dreams, and wishes. And these must be respected and responded to with great love, with great compassion, and with genuine tenderness.
>
> "We know that it is the prayer of your beloved, as it is the prayer of each of us here, that you will continuously light these candles of love, so that there will always be light and joy, peace and harmony in your hearts and in your home [each set their candles down].
>
> "Please kiss each other."

more ritual ideas

The following rituals are inspired by real couples' ceremonies. Borrow an idea
for your own wedding, or use these to help brainstorm your own new tradition.

TREE PLANTING

Planting a tree at your ceremony site is a perfect ritual for a garden wedding; work with your venue to see if it's allowed. You can either plant a small sapling during the ceremony itself, or have the tree planted beforehand and water the tree at the ceremony. As an extra touch, you can use soil from each of your childhood homes to plant the tree as well.

WINE BOX RITUAL

In this ritual, you'll both write letters to each other before the wedding. At the ceremony, place a bottle of wine, two wineglasses, and the letters inside the wine box—the box can be personalized ahead of time with engravings or fabric lining. Then both partners and their parents (and whoever else you wish to include) will pound a nail into the box, one after the other, to seal it. After the wedding, you have two options: either you can save the box and open it if you ever run into hard times, drinking the wine together and reading the letters; or you can open the box each year on your anniversary, drink the wine together, read the letters, and refill the box with new wine and new letters for the next year.

WINE CEREMONY

Set up two small carafes of wine (one white and one red), one empty large carafe, and two wineglasses at the altar. After exchanging vows, you both will take a small carafe of wine and pour it into the large carafe, blending the wines to represent your union. Then, pour each other a glass of the blended wine, and take a sip. Your officiant can lead the ritual with this script:

"Let the wine you each hold in your hands represent your individual lives. As you pour them together, see how the two halves become indistinguishable and forever indivisible. So your separate lives now become a whole life together. When you drink from your glasses now, and every time you share wine together from this day forward, remember your commitment to truth and honesty."

STONE BURYING

This ritual is perfect for a beach wedding. Sometime before the day, have a stone engraved with your initials, wedding date, and any special quotes or sayings. During the ceremony, bury the stone in the sand together while your officiant announces that sealing the stone under the sand represents your permanent commitment to each other.

STONE CEREMONY

At the end of your rehearsal dinner, distribute a smooth white stone and a permanent marker to each guest. Ask that everyone go home, write a short wish or piece of advice on the stone, and bring it to the wedding. Then during the ceremony, have these guests come up one by one and place their stones into a large vase or bowl.

DECLARATION OF SUPPORT

Get your guests involved with this unique idea. After you've said your own vows, have your officiant ask your guests to stand and pledge their support to you through good times and bad, asking them to seal their vow by saying "I will" in unison.

sand ceremony (hawaiian)

This ritual is said to have Hawaiian origins, but it has become popular for destination weddings in any location for its tropical vibe. In this ritual, each member of the couple pours his or her own vessel of sand (which is often color coded to represent each person) into a third, empty vessel to symbolize their marriage. The vessel with the mixed sand can be closed with a stopper and saved as a keepsake.

Your officiant can lead the ritual with this script:

"Today, this relationship is symbolized through the pouring of these two individual containers of sand, one, representing you, _____ , and all that you were, all that you are, and all that you will ever be, and the other representing you, _____ , and all that you were and all that you are, and all that you will ever be. As these two containers of sand are poured into the third container, the individual containers of sand will no longer exist, but will be joined together as one. Just as these grains of sand can never be separated and poured again into the individual containers, so will your marriage be."

crossing sticks (african american)

In an African American tradition that dates back to the time of slavery, couples demonstrate their commitment by crossing tall wooden sticks. The sticks represent the power and life force within trees. By crossing the sticks, the couple expresses a wish for a strong and grounded beginning. If you decide to incorporate this tradition, you can choose large branches from both of your families' homes or from a place meaningful to you as a couple.

jumping the broom (african american)

An African tribal ritual had couples placing sticks on the ground to symbolize their home together. This may be the origin of broom jumping, which was popular among African American slaves (who could not have official wedding ceremonies); it may also symbolize the sweeping away of evil spirits. The couple holds the broom together and sweeps in a circle while the officiant or a family elder talks about the significance of the ritual. Then the broom is placed on the floor and the couple joins hands. Everyone counts to three—then you jump!

Your officiant (or anyone really) can read this reworded version of a traditional slave marriage poem:

"Dark and stormy may come the weather,
This man and woman are joined together.
Let none but him that makes the thunder,
Put this man and woman asunder.
I therefore announce you both the same,
Be good, go long, and keep up your name.
The broomstick's jumped, the world's not wide,
She's now your own, go kiss your bride!"

tasting the four elements (yoruba)

In a ritual adapted from a Yoruba tradition, the bride and groom taste four flavors that represent different emotions within a relationship: sour (lemon), bitter (vinegar), hot (cayenne), and sweet (honey). By tasting each of the flavors, the couple symbolically demonstrates that they will be able to get through the hard times in life and, in the end, enjoy the sweetness of their marriage.

mala badol (bangladesh)

After the wedding feast, the ritual of Mala Badol is performed in Bangladesh and other South Asian countries. A thin cloth is placed over both the bride and the groom. They feed each other and share sips of *borhani* (a spicy yogurt drink) beneath the cloth. While looking at their reflection in a mirror, the bride and groom are asked, "What do you see?" They each answer with a romantic declaration, such as, "I see the rest of my life." The couple then exchanges garlands of flowers. Recently, a new custom of exchanging rings has been added to the ritual.

breaking the glass (jewish)

Crushing a wineglass under the groom's foot at the end of the ceremony is a Jewish tradition with many meanings. It's a symbol of the destruction of the First Temple in Jerusalem; a representation of the fragility of relationships; and a reminder that marriage changes the lives of individuals forever. Or interpret it this way: drinking the wine represents the joys and sweetness of life, and crushing the glass represents the hardships.

p'ye-baek (korea)

The bride offers dates and chestnuts—symbols of children—to the groom's parents while sitting at a low table covered with other symbolic offerings. The parents offer sake in return, and as a final gesture they throw the dates and chestnuts at the bride, who tries to catch them in her large wedding skirt. Although this ritual traditionally takes place a few days after the wedding, in the United States the *p'ye-baek* is often held right before the reception, with the bride and groom in full Korean costume. Family members may also offer gifts of money in white envelopes to the bride.

gifts of eggs (muslim)

Eggs, which represent fertility and righteousness in Islam, are often given to the couple as symbolic gifts. The bride and groom may be handed eggs and showered with rice, candy, and dried fruit as they leave the reception.

honey and walnuts (greece)

In some of the Greek islands, the wedding ceremony ends with honey and walnuts being offered to the bride and groom from silver spoons. Walnuts are chosen because they break into four parts, symbolizing the bride, the groom, and their two families.

Notes_____

_____

_____

_____

_____

_____

_____

_____

_____

_____

_____

_____

_____

_____

_____

_____

_____

_____

_____

_____

_____

_____

_____

_____

_____

_____

_____

_____

programs and quotes

They're not mandatory, but wedding programs are wonderful keepsakes, and they will keep your guests in the loop as to who your attendants are, what readings and pieces of music will be performed, and what rituals will be included (especially if they are ethnic or religious customs with which not all of your guests are familiar). You can even tell the story of how you met and fell in love, share baby pictures, or honor your deceased grandparents in a program. Here's what to consider when creating yours.

PROGRAMMING NOTES

Your program can be as simple as a single sheet of paper, as clever as words printed on a paper fan, or as complex as a bound, printed booklet. Most are somewhere in between, often with several pages folded over and stapled, or held together by ribbon.

A basic program includes the following:

- Your names—"The marriage of Anna Sinclair and Robert Dixon"—and the wedding date.

- The names of all the members of the wedding party. You may also choose to include each bridesmaid's and groomsman's relationship to you ("college friend of the groom").

- The names of your parents and your officiant.

- The names of friends and relatives who are reading or performing, as well as the titles of the poems, passages, or songs.

- The order of the ceremony so your guests can follow along. Include the names and writers/composers of the readings and songs used (you could also include the words of any poems that are read).

A more extended program may include:

- An explanation of any ethnic or religious rituals. Your officiant or a family member may be able to help you compose the words, or there may be a church or temple document you can borrow from. You don't need a four-page history, just enough to give people an idea of the ritual's overall significance.

- A heads-up for any specific instructions for guests (for example, most of a Quaker ceremony is silent, and guests are free to stand up at any time and say something to the couple).

- An "In Memoriam" for important family members who have passed away, or a special mention of those who are unable to attend. This can be done by writing a personal message or printing one of the honored person's favorite poems or songs. Many couples also thank their guests in the program.

- A recent photo of yourselves, pictures from your courtship, or favorite shots of the two of you as babies or children.

Programs should be handed out by ushers, by young assistants (a great role for those too-old-to-be-flower-girl types), or simply left on each seat (assign an attendant to the task).

MEANINGFUL AND FAMOUS QUOTES

Include a meaningful quote about love, life, or friendship on the cover of your program—or even incorporate one into your invitation—to symbolize your relationship. You may already know the words that exactly express who you two are together. If not, here are some ideas; many can also be used in toasts. Also look at the readings on pages 44–91 for lines to excerpt.

Knowledge of what is possible is the beginning of happiness.
—*George Santayana*

Who can doubt that we exist only to love? Disguise it, in fact, as we will, we love without intermission. . . . We live not a moment exempt from its influence.
—*Blaise Pascal*

Lindsey & Mike
MAY 28
COLORADO SPRINGS,
COLORADO

Lindsey and Mike wanted their programs to have a mostly classic look with a few unique touches. The cover was made of shimmering fabric topped with a calligraphed monogram. Inside, the program listed a special thank-you to Lindsey's and Mike's parents: "As we turn the page and begin the next chapter of our lives together, we will look at the examples that you have set for us."

a program template

Here's a sample program to get you started working on yours. It's for a straightforward, fold-over program that's made like a book, with one "spread" inside. Or you could also do it as a single flat page.

COVER

THE WEDDING OF

Katherine Emily Spade

AND

Bradley Steven Bartlett

OCTOBER 6
CHICAGO, ILLINOIS

NOTHING IS WORTH MORE
THAN THIS DAY.
~Goethe

PAGE 1

Our Wedding Party

MAID OF HONOR
Audra Spade, sister of the bride

BEST MAN
Kevin Bartlett, brother of the groom

BRIDESMAIDS
Kristin Meyer, cousin of the bride
Taylor Baldwin, friend of the bride
Kelly Scott, friend of the bride

GROOMSMEN AND
GROOMSWOMEN
David Bartlett, brother of the groom
Marcus Daly, friend of the groom
Karen Carson, friend of the groom

FLOWER GIRL
Carrie McDonnell, niece of the bride

PARENTS OF THE BRIDE
Kara and Colin Spade

PARENTS OF THE GROOM
Sandra Kincaid
Steven and Maria Bartlett

OFFICIANT
The Reverend Thomas Stevenson

READERS
Michael Bartlett, cousin of the groom
Gina Dawson, friend of the couple

Our Ceremony

PRELUDE
"Can't Help Falling in Love," Elvis Presley
"My Romance," Rosemary Clooney
"Just in Time," Frank Sinatra

PROCESSIONAL
"Canon in D," Pachelbel

WELCOME

READING
From *The Prophet*, by Kahlil Gibran

INTERLUDE
"At Last"
Sung by the groom

EXCHANGE OF VOWS AND RINGS

READING
"Give All to Love," by Ralph Waldo Emerson

*At this time, Kate and Brad will light
their unity candle from candles lit by their
mothers, Kara and Sandy. This represents the
joining of our two families and the
creation of our new family.*

RECESSIONAL
"All You Need Is Love," The Beatles

*Reception begins at 6:30 p.m. at
Oakwood Country Club. See you there!*

WE'D LIKE TO THANK
ALL OUR FAMILY AND
FRIENDS WHO ARE HERE
TODAY—AND WE REMEMBER
THOSE WHO CAN'T BE.

WE LOVE YOU ALL, AND IT
MEANS SO MUCH TO US TO
HAVE YOU SHARE IN OUR
WEDDING DAY.

~*Kate & Brad*

Love is an act of endless forgiveness, a tender look which becomes
a habit.
—*Peter Ustinov*

What do I get from loving you? Loving you.
—*John-Roger*

The goal of life should not be to find joy in marriage, but to bring more
love and truth into the world. We marry to assist each other in this task.
—*Leo Tolstoy*

To love someone is to see a miracle invisible to others.
—*François Mauriac*

That Love is all these, is all we know of Love.
—*Emily Dickinson*

Your embraces alone give life to my heart.
—*Ancient Egyptian saying*

You know you're in love when you can't fall asleep because reality is
finally better than your dreams.
—*Dr. Seuss*

In our life there is a single color, as on an artist's palette, which provides
the meaning of life and art. It is the color of love.
—*Marc Chagall*

A friend is someone who knows all about you and still loves you.
—*Elbert Hubbard*

Once upon a time there was a boy who loved a girl, and her laughter was
a question he wanted to spend his whole life answering.
—*Nicole Krauss, from* The History of Love

We are ordinarily so indifferent to people that when we have invested
one of them with the possibility of giving us joy, or suffering, it seems as
if he must belong to some other universe, he is imbued with poetry.
—*Marcel Proust,* Remembrance of Things Past

However rare true love is, true friendship is even rarer.
—*François duc de La Rochefoucauld*

Those alone are wise who know how to love.
—*Seneca*

The supreme happiness of life is the conviction that we are loved.
—*Victor Hugo*

Love, love, love—that is the soul of genius.
—*Wolfgang Amadeus Mozart*

To love is to place our happiness in the happiness of another.
—*Gottfried Wilhelm Leibniz*

We love because it's the only true adventure.
—*Nikki Giovanni*

Love is that condition in which the happiness of another person is essential to your own.
—*Robert A. Heinlein*

Two souls with but a single thought,
Two hearts that beat as one.
—*Freidrich Halm*

Love is all we have, the only way that each can help the other.
—*Euripides*

It is the true season of love when we know that we alone can love; that no one could ever have loved before us and that no one will ever love in the same way after us.
—*Johann Wolfgang von Goethe*

Being deeply loved by someone gives you strength, while loving someone deeply gives you courage.
—*Lao Tzu*

When one has once fully entered the realm of love, the world—no matter how imperfect—becomes rich and beautiful, it consists solely of opportunities for love.
—*Søren Kierkegaard*

Love will find a way.
—*Anonymous*

The greatest pleasure of life is love.
—*William Temple*

The greatest thing you'll ever learn is just to love and be loved in return.
—*From "Nature Boy," by Nat King Cole*

Marriage is serious business and hard work. It's not just becoming roommates, it's becoming soul mates; it's not just signing a license, it's sharing a life. . . . The words in the marriage ceremony "from this day forward" are scary. At the moment a couple exchanges those vows, they can never know what they really mean, what hills and valleys stretch out in front of them in the years ahead. But if you take the words seriously, there's no going back. There's only the future, unlimited and unknowable, and the promise to make the journey together.
—*Steve and Cokie Roberts,*
From the introduction to From This Day Forward

Love overcomes hate. Love has no color. Love has no orientation. All is love.
—*Adam Lambert*

Love is the joy of the good, the wonder of the wise, the amazement of the Gods.
—*Plato*

Love is friendship set on fire.
—*Jeremy Taylor*

Love is a taste of paradise.
—*Sholom Aleichem*

Love is like pi—natural, irrational, and very important.
—*Lisa Hoffman*

Marriage is the fusion of two hearts—the union of two lives—the coming together of two tributaries.
—*Peter Marshall*

Life is the flower of which love is the honey.
—*Victor Hugo*

Love doesn't make the world go 'round. Love is what makes the ride worthwhile.
—*Franklin P. Jones*

One love, one heart, one destiny.
—*Bob Marley*

I have found the paradox that if I love until it hurts, then there is no hurt, but only more love.
—*Mother Teresa*

When love reigns, the impossible may be attained.
—*Indian proverb*

Love is the greatest refreshment in life.
—*Pablo Picasso*

God created us so that we should form the human family, existing together because we were made for one another. We are not made for an exclusive self-sufficiency but for interdependence, and we break the law of being at our peril.
—*Desmond Tutu*

Who travels for love finds a thousand miles not longer than one.
—*Japanese proverb*

There is a single magic, a single power, a single salvation, and a single happiness, and that is called loving.
—*Hermann Hesse*

A life without love is like a year without summer.
—*Swedish proverb*

Love is the only gold.
—*Alfred, Lord Tennyson*

The best and most beautiful things in the world cannot be seen or even touched. They must be felt with the heart.
—*Helen Keller*

If you would marry wisely, marry your equal.
—*Ovid*

At the touch of love everyone becomes a poet.
—*Plato*

Harmony is pure love, for love is a concerto.
—*Lope de Vega*

Love is something eternal; the aspect may change, but not the essence.
—*Vincent van Gogh*

The only true gift is a portion of yourself.
—*Ralph Waldo Emerson*

We love the things we love for what they are.
—*Robert Frost*

Mutual love, the crown of bliss.
—*John Milton*

Never above you. Never below you. Always beside you.
—*Walter Winchell*

To love is to admire with the heart.
—*Théophile Gautier*

When the one man loves the one woman and the one woman loves the one man, the very angels desert heaven and sit in that house and sing for joy.
—*Brahma sutra*

What's mine is yours and what is yours is mine.
—*William Shakespeare,* Measure for Measure, *Act V*

Love demands all, and has a right to it.
—*Ludwig van Beethoven*

I don't want to live. I want to love first, and live incidentally.
—*Zelda Fitzgerald*

Love is the master key that opens the gates of happiness.
—*Oliver Wendell Holmes*

Friendship is the marriage of the soul.
—*Voltaire*

Marriage is the will of two to create the one who is more than those who created it.
—*Friedrich Nietzsche*

There is always some madness in love. But there is also always some reason in madness.
—*Friedrich Nietzsche*

This is love—to fly upward toward the endless heavens.
—*Rumi*

Love is, above all, the gift of oneself.
—*Jean Anouilh*

There is no remedy for love than to love more.
—*Henry David Thoreau*

Chief of all love's joys is in knowing we love each other.
—*George Eliot*

Love is you, you and me.
—*John Lennon*

To love and be loved is to feel the sun from both sides.
—*David Viscott*

When two people are at one in their inmost hearts, they shatter even the strength of iron or of bronze.
—*I Ching*

The meaning of marriage begins in the giving of words. We cannot join ourselves to one another without giving our word. And this must be an unconditional giving, for in joining ourselves to one another we join ourselves to the unknown. . . . You do not know the road; you have committed your life to a way.

—*Ralph Waldo Emerson*

I am nothing special, of this I am sure. I am a common man with common thoughts and I've led a common life. There are no monuments dedicated to me and my name will soon be forgotten, but I've loved another with all my heart and soul, and to me, this has always been enough.

—*Nicholas Sparks, from* The Notebook

Marriage is like a golden ring in a chain, whose beginning is a glance and whose ending is eternity.

—*Kahlil Gibran*

Megan & Niall

DECEMBER 31
SARASOTA SPRINGS,
NEW YORK

The programs were one of Megan's favorite details. For a timeless look, the booklets were printed on square pearl paper, and the cover was decorated with a classic wreath design (the satin ribbon at the top was meant to look like a bow). On the back, an old Irish toast gave tribute to Niall's heritage: "In the new year, may your hand be stretched out in friendship, and never in want."

Love keeps the cold out better than a cloak.
—*Henry Wadsworth Longfellow*

The only transformer and alchemist that turns everything into gold is love. The only magic against death, aging, ordinary life, is love.
—*Anaïs Nin,* The Diary of Anaïs Nin

Happy are they who enjoy an uninterrupted union, and whose love, unbroken by complaints, shall not dissolve until the last day.
—*Horace*

Love indeed is light from heaven, a spark of that immortal fire.
—*Lord Byron*

Deeper than speech our love,
Stronger than life our tether.
—*Rudyard Kipling*

There is nothing nobler or more admirable than when two people who see eye to eye keep house as man and wife, confounding their enemies and delighting their friends.
—*Homer,* The Odyssey

I love you. You're my only reason to stay alive . . . if that's what I am.
—The Twilight Saga: New Moon

It's love. It's not Santa Claus.
—(500) Days of Summer

If there were another life, I'd live it for her.
—*Andrea Bocelli, "Vivo Per Lei"*

In a wide sea of eyes
I see one pair that I recognize
And I know that I am
I am, I am the luckiest
—*Ben Folds, "The Luckiest"*

Love is too weak a word for what I feel—I luuuurve you, I loave you, I luff you, two Fs.
—*Woody Allen,* Annie Hall

Notes

music and dances

Make no mistake: well-selected wedding music is a must-have. In every culture, music is an important part of ritual—an inherent, practically crucial factor because of its ability to evoke emotion and bring people together. From the moment you walk down the aisle to the last dance at your reception, the songs you choose will color the day to make it uniquely yours (of course, you'll want a band or DJ you can depend on, but be sure you have major input on the music that's played).

THE CEREMONY

The music you choose guides your guests through the ceremony, pumps up the emotion of what's taking place, and expresses your perspective, whether it's religious, cultural, or personal. Select songs that have meaning for you, that give you goose bumps, or that simply make you groove—whether they're traditional walking-the-aisle tunes, sultry standards, or evocative ethnic vibrations. Here's how:

- Before you do anything else, decide your basic ceremony playlist structure. Typically, there are several selections for the prelude (before the wedding begins), a processional and recessional, plus one or two additional selections during the ceremony itself.

- Talk to your officiant. If you're having a religious ceremony, there may be guidelines and/or restrictions on the music you can play (for example, you may not be able to play secular tunes in some sanctuaries). Your officiant can offer you ideas and a starting point for choosing appropriate music.

- If it's possible for you to include secular music in your ceremony, consider whether you'll stick with classical music—traditional or not—or other types of tunes for walking the aisle. Another popular option is to play modern music on traditional instruments (like a string quartet version of your favorite rock song). Run your ideas by your officiant, if necessary.

- Next, figure out just where your ceremony music will be coming from—a church organist or pianist, perhaps with vocal accompaniment? a string quartet? a folk guitarist? a bagpiper? off an iPod? Members of the band you hire for your reception may be able to double as ceremony musicians, or your DJ may be able to play your selections if your ceremony will be held in the same place as your reception. Choose based on site restrictions (your church may dictate that their musical staff plays weddings) or the type of music you think you'd like.

great ceremony selections

When you think about wedding music, you probably think "Here Comes the Bride." It's probably the most famous processional song, and there are others that are commonly used by thousands of marrying couples every year. The following lists are suggestions for your ceremony music from the prelude to the recessional, including traditional selections and some not-so-traditional tunes that we think would be wonderful for the right wedding—maybe yours.

THE PRELUDE

Traditional/Classical

Brandenberg Concerto no. 3, Johann Sebastian Bach

Brandenberg Concerto no. 4, Johann Sebastian Bach

"Clair de lune," Claude Debussy

Concerto for Harpsichord in F Minor, 2nd movement, "Largo," Johann Sebastian Bach

"Courante" from *Three Lute Dances*, Ludwig van Beethoven

"La grace," Georg Telemann

"Largo," from *New World Symphony*, Antonin Dvorák

"O mio babbino caro," Giacomo Puccini

Prelude and Fugue in A, Johann Sebastian Bach

Prelude to Afternoon of a Faun, Claude Debussy

Carrie & Jared
MAY 24
MALIBU, CALIFORNIA

Carrie and Jared followed lots of Jewish wedding traditions: marrying beneath a huppah, reading their ketubah, and breaking the wineglass. But for their ceremony music, they went contemporary. A guitarist played all Beatles songs. The couple did finish the day with one Jewish musical tradition, however: the horah, a dance in which the bride and groom are hoisted aloft on chairs while guests form a circle around them.

CEREMONY MUSICIANS: QUESTIONS TO ASK

What are some good questions I can ask potential ceremony musicians?

When you talk to potential ceremony musicians, ask:

- Has he or she or the group done many weddings?

- Can you hear the musician play, either live or on a recording?

- What type of music does the musician specialize in? Does this agree with what you envision? Does the musician have sheet music, or is he/she willing to purchase music for a song you'd like?

- How does the musician handle the stopping and starting of songs during a wedding so that they sound natural, not cut off unexpectedly? (Does the song fade out seamlessly? Does the musician know precisely how long a version to play?)

- Will the musician bring his or her own equipment? Will anything else be needed (microphones, etc.)? Will they need amplification in your setting?

- If the musician will accompany in-house musicians at your site, is he or she available for a rehearsal?

- How much setup time will be needed?

- What is the musician's fee? Does he or she work by the hour?

Be sure to get written contracts from your ceremony musician(s), just as you would with any other wedding vendor, and consider whether you'll need the musician(s) present at your ceremony rehearsal. If you're having a long service with numerous musical selections, your officiant may want to talk to the musician(s) about cues, when to start and stop various pieces, and the like.

Sonata for Piano no. 4 in E-flat Major, 1st movement, "Adagio," Wolfgang Amadeus Mozart

Suite no. 3 for Orchestra, Johann Sebastian Bach

Symphony for Organ no. 5 in F Minor, op. 42, no. 1: 5th movement, "Toccata," Charles-Marie Widor

"Trio for Two Flutes and Harp," from *L'Enfance du Christ*, Hector Berlioz

Variations on a Theme of Haydn in B-flat Major, Johannes Brahms

Waltz in A-flat, Johannes Brahms

Water Music Suite no. 1 in F: "Air," George Handel

Water Music Suite no. 1 in F: "Menuet," George Handel

Wedding Cantata, Johann Sebastian Bach

Well-Tempered Clavier, Book 1: Prelude and Fugue no. 1 in C, Johann Sebastian Bach

Vintage

"Across the Universe," The Beatles
"At Last," Etta James
"Blue Skies," Ella Fitzgerald
"Chapel of Love," The Dixie Cups
"I've Got a Crush on You," Linda Ronstadt or Sarah Vaughan
"Just in Time," Frank Sinatra
"Let's Do It (Let's Fall in Love)," Louis Armstrong
"Longer," Dan Fogelberg
"L-O-V-E," Nat King Cole
"Love Theme from *Romeo and Juliet*," Henry Mancini
"My Funny Valentine," Eartha Kitt or Linda Ronstadt
"My Romance," Tony Bennett or Rosemary Clooney
Rhapsody in Blue, George Gershwin
"Watch What Happens," Frank Sinatra or Tony Bennett
"Wedding Song," Bob Dylan
"We've Only Just Begun," The Carpenters
"What a Wonderful World," Louis Armstrong
"You and I," Stevie Wonder
"You Make Me Feel So Young," Frank Sinatra
"You'd Be So Nice to Come Home To," Ella Fitzgerald or Frank Sinatra

Contemporary

"Beautiful Day," Vitamin String Quartet
"Better Together," Jack Johnson
"Everybody," Ingrid Michaelson
"Hey There Delilah," Plain White T's
"Home," Michael Bublé
"I Do," Colbie Caillat
"I Was Made for You," She & Him
"Mary May & Bobby," Joe Purdy
"Over the Rainbow," Israel Kamakawiwo'ole
"Question," Old 97's
"She Will Be Loved," Maroon 5
"Such Great Heights," Iron & Wine
"We're Going to Be Friends," The White Stripes
"Your Hand in Mine," Explosions in the Sky

whom to hire?

Here are the most popular choices for live performers:

- Pianist
- Organist
- Harp soloist
- Acoustic guitar soloist
- String duo (two violins, or violin and cello)
- String trio (two violins and cello)
- String quartet (two violins, viola, and cello)
- Flute trio (flute, violin, and cello)
- Jazz combo (a small group that might include string bass, guitar, saxophone, and piano)

THE PROCESSIONAL

Traditional/Classical

"Allemande," *G-Major Suite,* Johann Pachelbel

"Arioso," Johann Sebastian Bach

"Bridal Chorus," from *Lohengrin,* Richard Wagner

"Canon in D" for three violins and bass, Johann Pachelbel

"Carillon," Herbert Murrill

"Crown Imperial," Sir William Turner Walton

"Fanfare for the Common Man," Aaron Copland

Fantasia in G, Johann Sebastian Bach

"Jesu, Joy of Man's Desiring," Johann Sebastian Bach

"Majesty," Georg Telemann

"March," from *Scipio,* George Handel

"Musetta's Waltz," from *La bohème,* Giacomo Puccini

"Prelude to *Te Deum* in D Major," Marc-Antoine Charpentier

"Processional," William Mathias

Romance no. 2 in F, Ludwig van Beethoven

"Sinfonia," from *Wedding Cantata,* Johann Sebastian Bach

Sonata for Piano no. 14 in C-sharp Minor, op. 27, no. 2, "Moonlight": 1st movement, Ludwig van Beethoven

Suite for Orchestra no. 3 in D Major: "Air on the G string," Johann Sebastian Bach

Suite in D Major: "Trumpet Voluntary" ("Prince of Denmark's March"), Jeremiah Clarke

"Trumpet Tune," John Stanley

"Trumpet Tune and Air in D," Henry Purcell

Water Music Suite no. 2: "Andante allegro," George Handel

"Wedding March," Félix-Alexandre Guilmant

"Wedding March," from *Midsummer Night's Dream,* op. 61, Felix Mendelssohn

"Wedding March," from *The Marriage of Figaro,* Wolfgang Amadeus Mozart

"Wedding March," from *The Sound of Music,* Richard Rodgers and Oscar Hammerstein

Vintage

"Always," Ella Fitzgerald

"Autumn Leaves," Nat King Cole

"The Book of Love," Peter Gabriel

"Can't Help Falling in Love," Elvis Presley

"Everything I Have Is Yours," Billie Holiday

"Here Comes the Sun," The Beatles

"I've Been Loving You Too Long," Otis Redding

"*La vie en rose,*" Édith Piaf

"Maybe I'm Amazed," Paul McCartney

"Moon River," Frank Sinatra

"More Than Words," Extreme

"Morning Has Broken," Cat Stevens

"The Prayer," Céline Dion and Andrea Bocelli

"Once Upon a Time . . . Story Book Love," from *The Princess Bride,* Mark Knopfler

Contemporary

"All I Want Is You," Vitamin String Quartet

"Brighter Than Sunshine," Aqualung

"Can't Take My Eyes Off of You," Lauryn Hill

"Come Away with Me," Norah Jones

"Hallelujah," Vitamin String Quartet

"Just the Way You Are," Bruno Mars

"The Luckiest," Ben Folds

"Luna," The Smashing Pumpkins

"Marry Me," Train

"1, 2, 3, 4," Plain White T's

"The Only Exception," Paramore

"Reasons to Love You," Meiko

"Sea of Love," Cat Power

"Speechless," Michael Jackson

"You and I," Michael Bublé

"You and I," Ingrid Michaelson

ADDITIONAL CEREMONY SELECTIONS (VOCAL OR INSTRUMENTAL)

Traditional/Classical

"Alleluia," from *Exultate Jubilate,* Wolfgang Amadeus Mozart

"Amazing Grace," spiritual

"*Ave Maria,*" Franz Schubert

Concerto for Guitar in D Major: "Largo," Antonio Vivaldi

"*Dodi Li* (My Beloved Is Mine)," Song of Songs

"*Hanava Babanot* (Beautiful One)," Song of Songs

"*In dulci jubilo,*" Hieronymus Praetorius

"Let the Bright Seraphim," George Handel

"The Lord's Prayer," Albert Hay Malotte

"Love's Old Sweet Song," James Molloy

"Nearer My God to Thee," Lowell Mason

the latest wedding hits

For an always-up-to-date list of contemporary song selections for ceremony processionals, last dances, and everything in between, go to TheKnot.com/music.

"Now Thank We All Our God," traditional

"Pastoral Symphony: Pifa," from *The Messiah*, George Handel

"*Rêverie*," Claude Debussy

"Rock of Ages," Charles Ives

"*Salut d'amour*, op. 12," Sir Edward Elgar

"Sheep May Safely Graze," Johann Sebastian Bach

"Songs (4) for Female Voices, 2 Horns and Harp," Johannes Brahms

"What God Hath Done, Is Rightly Done," from Cantata no. 99, Johann Sebastian Bach

Vintage

"All of Me," Billie Holiday or Frank Sinatra

"Cantara," Dead Can Dance

"Evergreen," Barbra Streisand

"In My Life," The Beatles

"She's Got a Way," Billy Joel

"Somewhere," from *West Side Story*, Leonard Bernstein and Stephen Sondheim

"That's All," Mel Tormé or Sam Harris

"There Is Love (Wedding Song)," Noel Paul Stookey (versions by The Captain & Tennille or Petula Clark)

"True Love," Rebecca St. James

"You Are So Beautiful," Joe Cocker

"You'll Never Walk Alone," Aretha Franklin

Contemporary

"Into the Mystic," Van Morrison

"Make You Feel My Love," Adele

"Marry You," Bruno Mars

"Minuet," Mark Magnuson

"My Love for You Is Real," Ryan Adams

"Realize," Colbie Caillat

"Somewhere Only We Know," Keane

"This Year's Love," David Gray

"The Way I Am," Ingrid Michaelson

THE RECESSIONAL

Traditional/Classical

"Agincourt Hymn," John Dunstable

"Alla Hornpipe," from *Water Music Suite no. 2 in D Major*, George Handel

"Arrival of the Queen of Sheba," from *Solomon*, George Handel

Brandenberg Concerto no. 2, Johann Sebastian Bach
Concerto for Violin in E Major, "Primavera": 1st movement, "Allegro,"
    Antonio Vivaldi
"Cornation March," Sir William Turner Walton
"Grand March," from *Aida*, Giuseppe Verdi
"*Grande choeur dialogué*," Eugène Gigout
"*Marche héroïque*," Herbert Brewer
Music for the Royal Fireworks, no. 4, "La réjouissance," George Handel
"Ode to Joy (Joyful, Joyful, We Adore Thee)," from the Ninth Symphony,
    Ludwig van Beethoven
"Rejoicing," Georg Telemann
"Rondeau," Henry Purcell
Sonata in A Major, 1st movement, Felix Mendelssohn
"Spring," from *The Four Seasons*, Antonio Vivaldi
Suite de symphonies no. 1: 1st movement, "Rondeau," Jean-Joseph Mouret
Toccata in B Minor, Eugène Gigout
"*Transports de joie*" (no. 3 from *L'Ascension*), Olivier Messiaen
"Triumphal March," op. 53, no. 3, Edvard Grieg
"Trumpet Overture," from *Indian Queen*, Henry Purcell
"Tuba Tune in D Major," op. 15, Craig Sellar Lang
"We Thank Thee, Lord," Sinfonia in D Major, Canata no. 29, Johann
    Sebastian Bach

Vintage
"All You Need Is Love," The Beatles
"Benedictus," Simon and Garfunkel
"Everlasting Love," Howard Jones
"For Once in My Life," Stevie Wonder
"Go There with You," Steven Curtis Chapman
"Gotta Have Love," Yolanda Adams
"Happy Together," The Turtles
"(I've Had) The Time of My Life," from *Dirty Dancing*, Bill Medley and
    Jennifer Warnes
"Joy," George Winston
"Let's Face the Music and Dance," Fred Astaire or Diana Krall
"Love Me Do," The Beatles
"Love Will Keep Us Together," The Captain & Tennille
"Lovesong," The Cure
"Night and Day," Frank Sinatra
"When I'm Sixty-Four," The Beatles
"You Got the Love," The Source

cultural music and traditional instruments

Music is a wonderful way to include your ethnic heritage in your ceremony, too. Incorporate bagpipes, the sitar, the accordion, steel drums, even the banjo or ukulele into your selections. Think about having live musicians at your ceremony site—the drama can't be beat. Another personal idea: include traditional songs from your grandparents' or parents' countries of origin. Don't know where to find these tunes? Ask your elders, and search the Internet, of course, for options and local musicians.

Contemporary
"Beautiful Day," U2
"Brighter Than the Sun," Colbie Caillat
"Crazy Little Thing Called Love," Queen
"Dog Days Are Over," Florence + The Machine
"Grow Old With Me," The Postal Service
"Happily Ever After," Blu Cantrell
"Hello Sunshine," Super Furry Animals
"Home," Edward Sharpe & The Magnetic Zeros
"I'm Yours," Vitamin String Quartet
"Love You Madly," Cake
"Marry You," Bruno Mars
"No One," Alicia Keys
"Not Fade Away," Grateful Dead
"This Will Be Our Year," The Zombies

questions to ask your entertainment

What are some good questions I can ask potential
reception musicians or DJs?

When you talk to potential reception bands
or DJs, ask:

- Do they have a signature sound or style? Does it
  fit with what you want? (You may want to ask
  this when you call to make an appointment; if
  you want a swing band and this is a blues
  ensemble, save everyone some time.)

- Does the band or DJ work with a playlist? Can
  you choose what you want played from it?

- If you want additional selections not on the list,
  will they accommodate you?

- Does/can the bandleader or DJ serve as an MC
  for the event? Can they also keep quiet, if you
  prefer that?

- How many band members—that is, what types
  of ensembles—are available? If you're talking to

a DJ, does he or she work alone, with an
assistant, with another DJ, with "dancers" (if you
don't want additional entertainment, say so).

- Will the band or DJ bring all their equipment—
  do you need to supply anything?

- Have they worked at your site before/are they
  familiar with the acoustics there?

- How much time would they need to set up?

- Do they write breaks into their contract? Would
  they need meals during the party?

- How many hours does their fee cover? Are
  there packages? What about overtime costs?

- What do they wear?

Of course, sign a contract with your chosen
band/DJ.

"Walking on a Dream," Empire of the Sun
"You and Me," Dave Matthews Band
"You Are the Best Thing," Ray LaMontagne
"You're the World to Me," David Gray

THE RECEPTION

From cocktails through dinner and dancing the night away, we've got great ideas for your playlist, from old standards to eighties essentials. Of course, this is just the beginning: Your band or DJ's playlist, as well as your own music collection, will turn up lots of other, perhaps much more personal, ideas.

A caveat: When you're making up your playlist, keep your guests in mind. Maybe you and your fiancé adore samba, but does Uncle George, or even many of your friends? Be sure to keep their tastes in mind as well when you're deciding on your tunes. Yes, it's your day, but you're depending on your guests to keep the dance floor shaking! Consider including a few of your to-die-for tunes—the ones you two just can't live without—and varying the majority of the playlist to accommodate everyone.

reception music notes

- The big question: live music or recorded? You may instinctively be leaning toward one or the other—perhaps you love eighties music and just can't picture a band nailing a Culture Club song, or maybe you just can't fathom a black-tie wedding without a fourteen-piece band. Consider the style of your party: If you want ambience and entertainment as well as dancing throughout the evening, you need a band. If all you care about is a clublike atmosphere and serious dancing, go for a DJ. Also consider the space: a twelve-piece band needs elbow room. And ultimately, consider your budget: Bands are, for good reason, typically more expensive. Top DJs can be pretty pricey, too.

- Consider whether you want to hire a group for cocktails and another for the reception itself (if you will have a traditional luncheon or dinner reception). You could have a jazz combo playing during cocktails and dinner, then a DJ for dancing, or a few members of the reception orchestra playing during cocktails, or the DJ playing background music then.

first-dance songs

Okay, you only get to choose one first-dance song, and we've compiled too many choices! Standards have been performed by multiple artists over the years, so we've selected our favorite renditions; keep in mind that there may be many more versions. Can't decide? Any of these would also be great as dinner or dancing music later on in your reception.

BIG BAND/JAZZ STANDARDS

"All the Things You Are," Ella Fitzgerald or Tony Bennett
"All the Way," Frank Sinatra or Barry Manilow
"Always," Frank Sinatra or Sarah Vaughan and Billy Eckstine
"As Time Goes By," from *Casablanca*, Tony Bennett or Frank Sinatra
"At Last," Etta James
"Baby, I Do," Natalie Cole
"Be My Life's Companion," Louis Armstrong or Rosemary Clooney
"Because of You," Tony Bennett
"The Best Is Yet to Come," Frank Sinatra
"Body and Soul," Louis Armstrong
"Cheek to Cheek," Ella Fitzgerald or Fred Astaire
"Come Rain or Come Shine," Billie Holiday or Ray Charles
"Embraceable You," Nat King Cole or Frank Sinatra
"Everything I Have Is Yours," Billie Holiday
"A Fine Romance," Joe Derise
"Fly Me to the Moon," Frank Sinatra
"From This Moment On," Ella Fitzgerald
"How Do You Speak to an Angel," Dean Martin
"I Can't Give You Anything but Love," Louis Armstrong
"I'm Crazy 'Bout My Baby (And My Baby's Crazy 'Bout Me)," Louis Armstrong
"Inseparable," Natalie Cole
"Isn't It Romantic," Frank Sinatra
"It Had to Be You," Harry Connick Jr. or Frank Sinatra
"It's Love," Lena Horne
"I've Got the World on a String," Bing Crosby or Mel Tormé
"L-O-V-E," Nat King Cole
"The Man I Love," Billie Holiday or Ella Fitzgerald
"More," Bobby Darin
"More Than You Know," Billie Holiday
"My Baby Just Cares for Me," Nina Simone

"My One and Only Love," Louis Armstrong or Sting

"My Sweet," Louis Armstrong

"The Nearness of You," Maureen McGovern or Tom Jones

"One Moment Worth Years," Louis Armstrong

"Our Day Will Come," Ruby & The Romantics

"Our Love Is Here to Stay," Tony Bennett or Dinah Washington

"Prelude to a Kiss," Ella Fitzgerald or Johnny Mathis

"Someone to Watch Over Me," Etta James or Barbra Streisand

"Tender Is the Night," Tony Bennett

"That Old Black Magic," Mel Tormé or Sarah Vaughan

"The Song Is You," Frank Sinatra

"The Sunshine of Your Smile," Frank Sinatra

"The Very Thought of You," Billie Holiday or Nat King Cole

"The Way You Look Tonight," Bing Crosby or Frank Sinatra

"We Are in Love," Harry Connick Jr.

"What Is This Thing Called Love?" Rosemary Clooney or Nat King Cole

"When I Fall in Love," Nat King Cole or Tom Jones

"When Somebody Thinks You're Wonderful," Fats Waller

"You Do Something to Me," Frank Sinatra or Peggy Lee

"You Go to My Head," Tony Bennett or Frank Sinatra

"You Send Me," Aretha Franklin or Sam Cooke

"You Stepped Out of a Dream," Sarah Vaughan

"You're Getting to Be a Habit with Me," Frank Sinatra or Mel Tormé

"You're My Thrill," Lena Horne

"You're Nobody Till Somebody Loves You," Dean Martin

OLDIES

"All I Have to Do Is Dream," The Everly Brothers

"Baby, It's You," The Shirelles

"Be My Baby," The Ronettes

"Because," Dave Clark Five

"Born to Be with You," The Chordettes

"Can't Help Falling in Love," Elvis Presley

"Chances Are," Johnny Mathis

"Dedicated to the One I Love," The Shirelles

"Devoted to You," The Everly Brothers

"For the Love of You," The Isley Brothers

"For Your Precious Love," Jerry Butler and The Impressions

"God Only Knows," The Beach Boys

freshen up your first dance

Three new ways to add a little extra jazz to this tradition:

SURPRISING STYLE SWITCH

Shock your guests by starting with a slow dance and then switching to something fast and sexy or over-the-top silly. Imagine: An Etta James song morphs into Dr. Dre and 2Pac's "California Love."

HEAD-SPINNING MEDLEYS

Can't pick a song? Try a first-dance medley. If your feet can switch from "You Are the Sunshine of My Life" to "Livin' on a Prayer" to "You're the One That I Want," you can pack all your favorites into one dance.

IMPRESSIVE CHOREOGRAPHY

If you're dance-floor confident, ditch the traditional waltz for a highly choreographed routine. Don't have time to create a dance yourself? Copy the moves from a favorite music video or movie musical.

first-dance song tips

Many couples have "Our Song," and if it's appropriate for a first dance (that is, it's got a rhythm that you can dance to), your choice of first dance may be incredibly easy. But if it's not quite that clear, here are some ways to narrow down your favorite romantic tunes:

- Look through your music collection and pinpoint the albums you both like a lot. Check the song titles. Are there any romantic ones you both really enjoy that you'd feel comfortable dancing to? This doesn't have to be the song that transformed your relationship; it's fine to choose a sweet ditty you just like.

- Consider movie soundtracks. There are many "Love Themes from . . . ," and if a certain movie really touched both of you, its love theme may be just the song to dance to. If the song is from a movie with a not-so-romantic title, you don't have to count it out—just let your DJ or bandleader know not to mention the name, and avoid something like this: "Barbara and John will now dance their first dance to the theme song from *Dying Young*."

- Think about whether there's a song that perfectly pertains to your situation: "At Last" by Etta James if you were friends for a long time before you got together, for example, or "It Had to Be You" by Frank Sinatra if you've been together a long time or have otherwise "beat the odds" in your relationship.

- Many standards were performed by multiple artists; we've just listed suggested singers. For example, "You Do Something to Me" is a Cole Porter standard—but did you know that Sinéad O'Connor covered it? If you like a certain song, do a search for its title to see who's performed it. You might just find the perfect version.

- Don't be afraid to choose whatever song you think is perfect. We know that some songs (even some of the ones listed here) might sound a bit kitschy or weird for a wedding, but our point is that your first-dance song can truly be anything that has the right sentiment, and can also be something that shows off your sense of humor.

- Would you rather boogie down for your first dance as an official couple? True, most first-dance songs are slow and romantic, but if you want to pick up the pace a bit or do something a little more campy—tango, anyone?—that's fine.

"Good Feeling," The Violent Femmes
"A Groovy Kind of Love," The Mindbenders or Phil Collins
"I Love You, Yes I Do," The Platters
"I Only Have Eyes for You," The Flamingos or Art Garfunkel
"I Only Want to Be with You," Dusty Springfield or Vonda Shepard
"In the Still of the Night," The Five Satins
"Let It Be Me," Nina Simone or The Everly Brothers
"The Look of Love," Dusty Springfield
"Love Is All Around," The Troggs
"Love Me Tender," Elvis Presley

"Memories Are Made of This," Dean Martin

"My Eyes Adored You," Frankie Valli

"My Girl," The Temptations

"My Own True Love," The Duprees

"Only You," The Platters

"Ooo Baby Baby," Smokey Robinson and The Miracles

"Sea of Love," Phil Phillips and The Twilights or The Honeydrippers

"Smile," Nat King Cole

"Stand By Me," Ben E. King

"That's How Strong My Love Is," Otis Redding

"To Know Him Is to Love Him," The Teddy Bears

"To Love Somebody," The Bee Gees

"Unforgettable," Nat King Cole

"Warm and Tender Love," Percy Sledge

"Wouldn't It Be Nice," The Beach Boys

"You Are the Sunshine of My Life," Stevie Wonder

"You Belong to Me," The Duprees or Patsy Cline

"You Send Me," Sam Cooke

"You Were Made for Me," Sam Cooke

"You'll Never Walk Alone," Elvis Presley

"(You're My) Soul and Inspiration," The Righteous Brothers

ROCK/INDIE/POP

"After All," Peter Cetera and Cher

"After All Is Said and Done," Beyoncé

"All I Want Is You," U2

"All My Love," Led Zeppelin

"Amazed," Lonestar

"And I Love Her," The Beatles

"Angel in the Snow," Elliott Smith

"Anyone Else but You," Moldy Peaches

"As Long As You Love Me," Backstreet Boys

"As Long As You Love Me," Justin Bieber and Big Sean

"Babe," Styx

"Baby, Come to Me," James Ingram featuring Patti Austin

"Baby, I Love Your Way," Peter Frampton

"Best of My Love," The Eagles

"Biggest Part of Me," Ambrosia

"Breathe," Faith Hill

"Change the World," Eric Clapton

"Chasing Cars," Snow Patrol

"Cherish," Kool & the Gang

"Color My World," Chicago

"Come What May," from *Moulin Rouge*

"Completely," Michael Bolton

"Count on Me," Bruno Mars

"Crash into Me," Dave Matthews Band

"Crazy for You," Madonna

"Crazy Love," Van Morrison

"Don't Know Much," Linda Ronstadt and Aaron Neville

"Don't Know Why," Norah Jones

"Eternal Flame," The Bangles

"Everything," Michael Bublé

"Faithfully," Journey

"Falling into You," Céline Dion

"Fields of Gold," Sting

"First Day of My Life," Bright Eyes

Meggie & Buck
MARCH 28
CAVE SPRING, GEORGIA

Meggie and Buck chose their first-dance song, "Have I Told You Lately," by Van Morrison, because of its special meaning to them as a couple. After they exchanged their first "I love you's" while dating, Buck started saying "Have I told you?" in lieu of saying "I love you." Meggie would always respond, "Lately?" The couple still says it to each other frequently and even had the phrase engraved inside Buck's wedding ring.

"Forever," Ben Harper

"Forever in My Life," Prince

"Giving You the Rest of My Life," Bob Carlisle

"Go There with You," Steven Curtis Chapman

"Grow Old with Me," John Lennon or Mary Chapin Carpenter

"Have I Told You Lately That I Love You," Van Morrison or Rod Stewart

"Head over Feet," Alanis Morrisette

"Here We Are," Gloria Estefan

"Heroes," David Bowie

"Hold My Hand," Hootie & the Blowfish

"Home," Edward Sharpe & The Magnetic Zeros

"How Much I Feel," Ambrosia

"How Sweet It Is to Be Loved by You," James Taylor

"I Believe in You and Me," Whitney Houston

"I Can Only Imagine," David Guetta and Chris Brown

"I Get Weak," Belinda Carlisle

"I Knew I Loved You," Savage Garden

"I Love You," Climax Blues Band

"I Remember You," Björk

"I Want to Know What Love Is," Foreigner

"I Will," The Beatles

"I Will Always Love You," Whitney Houston

"Ice Cream," Sarah McLachlan

"I'll Always Love You," Taylor Dayne

"I'll Have to Say I Love You in a Song," Jim Croce

"I'm Your Angel," Céline Dion and R. Kelly

"I'm Yours," Jason Mraz

"In My Life," The Beatles

"In Your Eyes," Peter Gabriel

"It Must Be Love," Madness

"It's All Coming Back to Me Now," Céline Dion

"Just Between You and Me," April Wine

"Just the Way You Are," Billy Joel

"Kiss Me," Sixpence None the Richer

"Lady," Styx

"Let Love Rule," Lenny Kravitz

"Let Me Love You," Ne-Yo

"Love Me Like the World Is Ending," Ben Lee

"Love Song," Tesla

"Love Will Keep Us Alive," The Eagles

"Lovesong," The Cure

real brides' inspired first-dance choices

Our song has always been "When She Believes," by Ben Harper. But during the planning process, Yair wasn't sure it would make a good first-dance song, so we picked another song that was easier to dance to. But Yair surprised me the night of the wedding by telling the DJ to play "When She Believes" for our first dance. It was so romantic and sweet!

—*Julia*

We went to see the band Bright Eyes play a few weeks before the wedding, which was a great date and a little break from all of the planning for us. We ended up dancing to "First Day of My Life" by Bright Eyes—it is such a sweet song.

—*Angela*

Half of our engagement was spent long-distance, as I was in Dubai for work. There was a TV commercial out at the time that featured the song "Fly Me Away," by Little and Ashley, that he said always made him think of me while we were apart. It's a very sweet and playful song that really captures our relationship.

—*Yasmin*

Our first-dance song was "Friday I'm in Love," by The Cure. Unconventional, but we both loved the song and we married on a Friday, and we are in love, so . . . Our contemporaries loved it, but our parents were a little taken aback by the words ("Wednesday, Thursday, heart attack . . .").

—*Donna*

My husband, Mark, and I chose a reggae song by a guy nobody knows called Finley Quaye. We had listened to him endlessly on a vacation in St. John about a year before we got married, and we often sang to and danced with each other to one of his songs called "Your Love Gets Sweeter Every Day." The guests at our wedding looked a little surprised when the band started to play a reggae number for our first dance, but shortly everyone—with or without a partner—was grooving on the dance floor along with us and smiling like crazy.

—*Leslie*

Brett and I got a Shania Twain album one day and listened to it in the car. We pulled up to a red light, and "From This Moment On" came on. We both fell silent and looked at each other, me with tears in my eyes. We kissed and we just knew that this was our wedding song. The moment was perfect—until people behind us honked because the light had turned green!

—*Alison*

Our first dance was to Stevie Wonder's "As," which we'd chosen not just for the romantic words, but because it starts out slow and gets faster. As soon as the music picked up, we had the DJ tell everyone to join us on the floor. We had instructed certain friends and family (before the wedding) to lead the others in just dancing "freestyle," though Jeff and I continued in the slow-dance fashion. It really felt like everyone was dancing in celebration this way, instead of just a mass "couples' dance" to our song.

—*Amy*

Our first-dance song was very unique. We were engaged in Central Park on a rock next to the water where everyone rides rowboats. When we went back to that very spot months later, That Guitar Man from Central Park was performing. There were hundreds of people, but we found a spot on our engagement rock. He started to talk about the most romantic song ever written and how he loved it so much that he included it on his new CD. He started singing "The Way You Look Tonight" and Joe and I just looked at each other. I knew right then that that was our song. We bought his CD a few weeks later, and That Guitar Man from Central Park serenaded us at our wedding.

—*Dana*

"Lucky," Jason Mraz

"Make It with You," Bread

"Make You Feel My Love," Adele

"Maybe I'm Amazed," Paul McCartney

"A Moment Like This," Kelly Clarkson

"More Than I Can Say," Leo Sayer

"My All," Mariah Carey

"My Heart Will Go On," Deline Dion

"My Love Is Your Love," Whitney Houston

"Never Gonna Let You Go," Sérgio Mendes

"No Ordinary Love," Sade

"Nobody Does It Better," Carly Simon

"Nothing's Gonna Change My Love for You," Glenn Medeiros

"Nothing's Gonna Stop Us Now," Starship

"Now That I Found You," Michael Bolton

"Old Fashioned," Cee Lo Green

"On the Wings of Love," Jeffrey Osborne

"Open Arms," Journey

"The Power of Love," Céline Dion

"Save the Best for Last," Vanessa Williams

"She's All I Ever Had," Ricky Martin

"She's an Angel," They Might Be Giants

"Sign Your Name," Terence Trent D'Arby

"Slave to Love," Bryan Ferry

"Somebody," Depeche Mode

"Something in the Way She Moves," James Taylor

"Something So Right," Paul Simon or Annie Lennox

"Stand By My Woman," Lenny Kravitz

"Steady As We Go," Dave Matthews Band

"Suddenly," Billy Ocean

"Sweet Thing," Van Morrison

"Take My Breath Away," Berlin

"Thumper," Mumford & Sons

"Time in a Bottle," Jim Croce

"Tonight and Forever," Carly Simon

"Trouble Me," 10,000 Maniacs

"True Companion," Marc Cohn

"Truly," Lionel Richie

"Truly Madly Deeply," Savage Garden

"2 Become 1," Spice Girls

"Us," Regina Spektor

"Vision of Love," Mariah Carey

"Waiting for a Girl Like You," Foreigner

"The Way I Am," Ingrid Michaelson

"We Belong," Pat Benatar

"We've Got Tonight," Bob Seger & The Silver Bullet Band

"When I Need You," Leo Sayer

"When I'm with You," Sheriff

"Will You Marry Me?" Vonda Shepard

"Woman," John Lennon

"Wonderful Tonight," Eric Clapton

"Written in the Stars," Elton John and LeAnn Rimes

"You and I," Ingrid Michaelson

"You and I," Lady Gaga

"You and I," Wilco

"You Are the Best Thing," Ray LaMontagne

"You Give Good Love," Whitney Houston

"Your Love Is King," Sade

"Your Song," Elton John

"You're in My Heart," Rod Stewart

"You're My Best Friend," Queen

"You're My Home," Billy Joel

"You're the Inspiration," Chicago

"You've Made Me So Very Happy," Blood, Sweat & Tears

MOTOWN/R&B/SOUL

"Ain't No Mountain High Enough," Ashford & Simpson

"Ain't No Stoppin' Us Now," McFadden & Whitehead

"Ain't No Woman (Like the One I Got)," The Four Tops

"Ain't Nobody," Chaka Khan

"Ain't Nothing Like the Real Thing," Aretha Franklin

"All My Life," K-Ci & Jo Jo

"Always and Forever," Heatwave

"Angel of Mine," Monica

"Back at One," Brian McKnight

"Beautiful," Mary J. Blige

"Being with You," Smokey Robinson

"Best Thing That Ever Happened to Me," Gladys Knight & The Pips

"Can't Get Enough of Your Love, Babe," Barry White

"Can't Take My Eyes Off You," Lauryn Hill

"Caught Up in the Rapture," Anita Baker

"Could It Be I'm Falling in Love," The Spinners

"Ebony Eyes," Rick James with Smokey Robinson

"Everything," Mary J. Blige

"Feel Like Makin' Love," Roberta Flack

"The First Time Ever I Saw Your Face," Roberta Flack

"Giving You the Best That I've Got," Anita Baker

"Here and Now," Luther Vandross

"I Do It for You (Everything I Do)," Brandy

"I Just Can't Stop Loving You," Michael Jackson

"I'll Be There," The Jackson 5

"I'll Take Care of You," Marvin Gaye

"I.O.U. Me," BeBe & CeCe Winans

"Just the Two of Us," Grover Washington Jr.

"Kissing You," Keith Washington

"Knocks Me Off My Feet," Stevie Wonder

"Let's Get It On," Marvin Gaye

"Let's Stay Together," Al Green

"Look What You Done for Me," Al Green

"Love and Happiness," Al Green

"My Cherie Amour," Stevie Wonder

"Never Knew Love Like This Before," Stephanie Mills

"Nothing Can Change This Love," Otis Redding

"On Bended Knee," Boyz II Men

"The Only One for Me," Brian McKnight

"Overjoyed," Stevie Wonder

"Shining Star," The Manhattans

"Since I Fell for You," Al Jarreau

"So Amazing," Luther Vandross

"So This Is Love," James Ingram

"Solid (As a Rock)," Ashford & Simpson

"Spend My Life with You," Eric Benet

"Still," The Commodores

"Sweet Love," Anita Baker

"Sweet Thing," Rufus featuring Chaka Khan

"The Sweetest Thing," Lauryn Hill

"That's the Way Love Goes," Janet Jackson

"This Will Be (An Everlasting Love)," Natalie Cole

"Tonight I Celebrate My Love," Roberta Flack and Peabo Bryson

"True Love," Calvin Richardson and Chico DeBarge

"We're in This Love Together," Al Jarreau

"You Are My Lady," Freddie Jackson

"You Make Me Feel Brand New," The Stylistics

"You Mean the World to Me," Toni Braxton
"You're All I Need to Get By," Marvin Gaye and Tami Terrell
"You're Makin' Me High," Toni Braxton

COUNTRY
"All I Have," Beth Nielsen Chapman
"All I Need to Know," Kenny Chesney
"Amazed," Lonestar
"Begin Again," Taylor Swift
"Blown Away," Carrie Underwood
"Darlin' Companion," Johnny Cash and Emmylou Harris
"Feels So Right," Alabama
"Forever and Ever, Amen," Randy Travis
"Friends for Life," Debby Boone
"God Must Have Spent a Little More Time on You," Alabama
"Here, There, and Everywhere," Emmylou Harris
"I Cross My Heart," George Strait
"I Do," Paul Brandt
"I Love the Way You Love Me," John Michael Montgomery
"I Love You," Martina McBride
"I Swear," John Michael Montgomery
"I Will Always Love You," Dolly Parton
"If Tomorrow Never Comes," Garth Brooks
"I'll Be There for You," Kenny Rogers
"I'll Still Be Loving You," Restless Heart
"I'll Take Care of You," Dixie Chicks
"In This Life," Collin Raye
"Islands in the Stream," Kenny Rogers and Dolly Parton
"A Long and Lasting Love," Crystal Gayle
"Love of My Life," Sammy Kershaw
"Love Story," Taylor Swift
'Lovin' You Is Fun," Easton Corbin
"Made for Lovin' You," Doug Stone
"The Man in Love with You," George Strait
"Me and You," Kenny Chesney
"Musta Had a Good Time," Parmalee
"No Place That Far," Sara Evans
"Ours," Taylor Swift
"Pledging My Love," Emmylou Harris

"She Believes in Me," Kenny Rogers

"Something to Talk About," Bonnie Raitt

"That's Our Kind of Love," Lady Antebellum

"There's No Love Like Our Love," Crystal Gayle and Gary Morris

"The Vows Go Unbroken (Always True to You)," Kenny Rogers

"What a Difference You've Made in My Life," Ronnie Milsap

"When Love Finds You," Vince Gill

"You and I," Eddie Rabbitt and Crystal Gayle

"You Decorated My Life," Kenny Rogers

"Your Love Amazes Me," John Berry

"You're So Beautiful," John Denver

"You're the One," The Oak Ridge Boys

"You've Got a Way," Shania Twain

first-dance cover songs

Sometimes the original is just too predictable. Here's a list of familiar first-dance songs with a twist:

"Across the Universe," Rufus Wainwright (original by The Beatles)

"At Last," Beyoncé (original by Etta James)

"The Best Is Yet to Come," Tony Bennett (original by Frank Sinatra)

"Can't Help Falling in Love," Ingrid Michaelson (original by Elvis Presley)

"Crazy in Love," Snow Patrol (original by Beyoncé)

"Crazy Love," Michael Bublé (original by Van Morrison)

"Grow Old with Me," The Postal Service (original by John Lennon)

"Heaven," DJ Sammy (original by Bryan Adams)

"Here Comes the Sun," Nina Simone (original by George Harrison)

"I Melt with You," Nouvelle Vague (original by Modern English)

"L-O-V-E," Joss Stone (original by Nat King Cole)

"No Ordinary Love," Deftones (original by Sade)

"To Love Somebody," Damien Rice and Ray LaMontagne (original by The Bee Gees)

"That's How Strong My Love Is," The Rolling Stones (original by Otis Redding)

"The Way You Look Tonight," Harry Connick Jr. (original by Fred Astaire)

"Wild Horses," The Sundays (original by The Rolling Stones)

"You Belong to Me," Carla Bruni (original by The Duprees)

"Your Song," Ewan McGregor (original by Elton John)

FROM MOVIES AND SHOWS

"All I Ask of You," from *The Phantom of the Opera*, Andrew Lloyd Webber

"As Long As You're Mine," from *Wicked*, Stephen Schwartz

"At the Beginning," from *Anastasia*, Richard Marx and Donna Lewis

"Best That You Can Do," from *Arthur*, Christopher Cross

"Can You Feel the Love Tonight," from *Lion King*, Elton John

"Can You Read My Mind," from *Superman*, John Williams

"(Everything I Do) I Do It for You," from *Prince of Thieves*, Bryan Adams

"Falling Slowly," from *Once*, Glen Hansard

"Give In to Me," from *Country Strong*, Billy Falcon, Rose Falcon, Elisha Hoffman

"Glory of Love," from *Karate Kid II*, Peter Cetera

"I Don't Want to Miss a Thing," from *Armageddon*, Aerosmith

"I Finally Found Someone," from *The Mirror Has Two Faces*, Barbra Streisand and Bryan Adams

"If I Loved You," from *Carousel*, Richard Rodgers and Oscar Hammerstein

"The Last Night of the World," from *Miss Saigon*, Alain Boublil and Claude-Michel Schönberg

kitschy classics

Some first-dance tunes are totally over the top—but maybe that's exactly what you want! Here are a few of our favorite superdrippy songs:

"Can You Feel the Love Tonight," Elton John

"Could I Have This Dance?" Anne Murray

"Could It Be Magic," Barry Manilow

"Endless Love," Diana Ross and Lionel Richie

"I Got You Babe," Sonny & Cher or UB40 and Chrissie Hynde

"I Honestly Love You," Olivia Newton-John

"Marry Me," Neil Diamond and Buffy Lawson

"On the Wings of Love," Jeffrey Osborne

"Sometimes When We Touch," Dan Hill

"Time After Time," Cyndi Lauper

"Unchained Melody," The Righteous Brothers

"What the World Needs Now," Jackie DeShannon

"Woman in Love," Barbra Streisand

"You Light Up My Life," Debby Boone

"You'll Be in My Heart," Phil Collins

"Love Came for Me," from *Splash*, Placido Domingo

"Love Makes the World Go 'Round," from *Carnival*, Bob Merrill

"Love Song for a Vampire," from *Bram Stoker's Dracula*, Annie Lennox

"Love Theme," from *Superman*, John Williams

"My Heart Will Go On," from *Titanic*, Céline Dion

"Once Upon a Time . . . Story Book Love," from *Princess Bride*, Mark Knopfler

"One Hand, One Heart," from *West Side Story*, Leonard Bernstein and Stephen Sondheim

"Only You," from *Starlight Express*, Andrew Lloyd Webber and Richard Stilgoe

"People Will Say We're in Love," from *Oklahoma*, Richard Rodgers and Oscar Hammerstein

"Seasons of Love," from *Rent*, Jonathan Larson

"So Close," from *Enchanted*, Jon McLaughlin

"So in Love," from *Kiss Me, Kate*, Cole Porter

"Someone Like You," from *Jekyll & Hyde*, Frank Wildhorn

"Till There Was You," from *The Music Man*, Meredith Wilson

"They Say It's Wonderful," from *Annie Get Your Gun*, Irving Berlin

"Up Where We Belong," from *An Officer and a Gentleman*, Joe Crocker and Jennifer Warnes

"We Belong Together," from *Toy Story 3*, Randy Newman

"When You Believe," from *Prince of Egypt*, Whitney Houston and Mariah Carey

"A Whole New World," from *Aladdin*, Regina Belle and Peabo Bryson

"Why Do I Love You?" from *Showboat*, Jerome Kern and Oscar Hammerstein

REGGAE

"Baby, I Love Your Way," Big Mountain

"Do It Sweet," Jackie Edwards

"Is This Love," Bob Marley & The Wailers

"Love Me Forever," Dennis Brown

"Love You Baby," Barry Biggs

"Me Love She," Mad Cobra & Tricia

"Souls Keep Burning," Dennis Brown

"When I Get Your Love," Chaka Demus & Pliers

parent dances

You two may choose to dance with your parents—usually, the bride with her father and/or the groom with his mother. The following are songs appropriate for these dances, but you may choose something completely different that is meaningful to you and your parent for a very personal reason. Or leave it to your parent to choose the song he or she would enjoy dancing to with you.

"Beautiful Boy (Darling Boy)," John Lennon
"Because You Loved Me," Céline Dion
"Butterfly Kisses," Bob Carlisle
"Child of Mine," Carole King
"Come Fly with Me," Frank Sinatra
"Daddy's Hands," Holly Dunn
"Daddy's Little Girl," The Mills Brothers or Al Martino
"Daughter," Loudon Wainwright III

Ede & Morgan
SEPTEMBER 5
SANTA FE, NEW MEXICO

Two things were most important to Ede and Morgan when planning their wedding: showing off the city of Santa Fe (Ede is from New Mexico) and the music. To pull it off, they made sure to have a mariachi band lead the guests from the ceremony to the reception—a Santa Fe tradition, Ede says. Then at the party, a soul band that the couple flew in from Tennessee kept guests on the dance floor all night.

"Good Riddance (Time of Your Life)," Green Day

"The Greatest Man I Never Knew," Reba McEntire

"How Sweet It Is (To Be Loved by You)," Marvin Gaye or James Taylor

"I Just Called to Say I Love You," Stevie Wonder

"I Learned from You," Miley Cyrus

"I Loved Her First," The Heartland

"I Turn to You," Christina Aguilera

"I Will Remember You," Sarah McLachlan

"If I Could," Regina Belle or Nancy Wilson

"I'll Be There," Jackson 5

"I'll Stand By You," The Pretenders

"Isn't She Lovely," Stevie Wonder

"Kind & Generous," Natalie Merchant

"Lean on Me," Bill Withers

"Let Him Fly," Dixie Chicks

"Little Star," Madonna

"Mama," Spice Girls

"Mama Don't Let Your Babies Grow Up to Be Cowboys," Willie Nelson

"My Father's Eyes," Amy Grant

"My Girl," The Temptations

"The River," Garth Brooks

"A Song for Mama," Boyz II Men

"Stealing Cinderella," Chuck Wicks

"Summer Wind," Frank Sinatra

"Sweet Potato Pie," Ray Charles

"The Sweetest Days," Vanessa Williams

"Thank Heaven for Little Girls," from *Gigi*, Frederick Loewe and Alan Jay Lerner

"Think of Me," from *The Phantom of the Opera*, Andrew Lloyd Webber

"The Times of Your Life," Paul Anka

"Turn Around," Harry Belafonte

"Unforgettable," Nat King Cole and/or Natalie Cole

"The Way We Were," Barbra Streisand

"Wind Beneath My Wings," Bette Midler

"You Are the Sunshine of My Life," Stevie Wonder

"You're My Best Friend," Queen

"You're the Inspiration," Chicago

"You've Got a Friend," James Taylor

"You've Got a Friend in Me," Randy Newman

dinner music

When it comes to music during the cocktail hour and/or the meal, the main word to keep in mind is *mellow*. Standards and bossa nova are great for this, but there are pop songs that are appropriate, too. Many of the songs on our first-dance list and contemporary ceremony music lists would also work. And just about all this dinner music would be great for slow dancing as well.

BIG BAND/JAZZ STANDARDS
"As Time Goes By," Tony Bennett or Engelbert Humperdinck
"Bewitched, Bothered, and Bewildered," Ella Fitzgerald or Linda
    Ronstadt
"Dream a Little Dream of Me," The Mamas and the Papas or Dean
    Martin
"Fly Me to the Moon," Frank Sinatra
"I Get a Kick Out of You," Tony Bennett or Shirley Bassey
"I've Got a Crush on You," Linda Ronstadt
"I've Got My Love to Keep Me Warm," Ella Fitzgerald
"I've Got You Under My Skin," Frank Sinatra
"Misty," Bing Crosby or Johnny Mathis
"One for My Baby," Fred Astaire or Tony Bennett
"The Shadow of Your Smile," Frank Sinatra or Rosemary Clooney
"Stardust," Harry Connick Jr. or Nat King Cole
"'Swonderful," Ella Fitzgerald
"That's Amore," Dean Martin
"They Can't Take That Away from Me," Ella Fitzgerald and Louis
    Armstrong
"Time After Time," Tony Bennett
"The Way You Look Tonight," Frank Sinatra or Mel Tormé
"What a Little Moonlight Can Do," Billie Holiday
"You Made Me Love You," Patsy Cline

OLDIES/SHOW TUNES
"Blue Velvet," Bobby Vinton
"Crazy," Patsy Cline
"Fever," Peggy Lee
"Love Me Tender," Elvis Presley
"Moon River," from *Breakfast at Tiffany's*, Henry Mancini
"On the Street Where You Live," from *My Fair Lady*, Frederick Loewe
    and Alan Jay Lerner
"Smoke Gets in Your Eyes," The Platters

"Some Enchanted Evening," from *South Pacific*, Richard Rodgers and
   Oscar Hammerstein
"This Magic Moment," The Drifters

ROCK/INDIE/POP
"Alison," Elvis Costello
"Blue," LeAnn Rimes
"Don't Dream It's Over," Crowded House
"Have You Ever Really Loved a Woman?" Bryan Adams
"Holding Back the Years," Simply Red
"I Second That Emotion," Smokey Robinson & The Miracles
"Moondance," Van Morrison
"Paradise," Coldplay
"Reminiscing," Little River Band
"Smooth Operator," Sade
"True," Spandau Ballet
"*Viva la vida*," Coldplay

BOSSA NOVA/BRAZILIAN
"*Aquarela do Brasil*," Toots Thielemans and Elis Regina
"*Baia*," Walter Wanderley
"*Corcovado* (Quiet Nights of Quiet Stars)," Astrud Gilberto
"*Desafinado* (Slightly Out of Tune)," Antônio Carlos Jobim or Gal Costa
"Girl from Ipanema," Astrud Gilberto or Antônio Carlos Jobim
"*Más qué nada*," Tamba Trio or Luís Henrique
"*Os grilos*," Marcos Valle
"*Triste*," Elis Regina

dancing music: songs to get the party moving

You'll want great slow and fast tunes to keep the party fresh. Choose
smooth grooves from the first-dance and dinner music lists to supple-
ment the tripping tunes from the following list. From disco to soul, new
wave to rock and roll, don't be afraid to mix it up!
"Addicted to Love," Robert Palmer
"Ain't No Stopping Us Now," McFadden & Whitehead
"Ain't Too Proud to Beg," The Temptations
"All I Wanna Do," Sheryl Crow
"All Shook Up," Elvis Presley
"American Pie," Don McLean

"Another Night," M.C. Sar and The Real McCoy

". . . Baby One More Time," Britney Spears

"Bad Romance," Lady Gaga

"Beat It," Michael Jackson

"Believe," Cher

"Best of My Love," The Emotions

"Billie Jean," Michael Jackson

"Bizarre Love Triangle," New Order

"Boogie Oogie Oogie," A Taste of Honey

"Boogie Wonderland," Earth, Wind & Fire

"Boogie Woogie Bugle Boy," Bette Midler

"Boom Boom Pow," Black Eyed Peas

cultural reception dances

Many cultures have their own traditional dances of celebration. You may want to include at your reception one that reflects your background or your new spouse's background. To find out more about your culture's dancing customs, ask your parents and grandparents. You'll probably find that the elders in your family are founts of wisdom on this subject!

THE HORAH

The horah is a traditional Jewish dance that culminates in the bride and groom being raised up on chairs by their peers. If you want to incorporate a lot of traditional Jewish music into your ceremony, consider hiring a klezmer band for the entire party or several hours of it. You can be assured every wedding band can do a rendition of the horah—it's even becoming popular at non-Jewish weddings.

THE TARANTELLA

The tarantella originated in southern Italy; it's a couple's dance that increases in speed, typically accompanied by castanets and a tambourine.

THE HIGHLAND FLING

This high-energy Scottish dance was supposedly used to test a warrior's strength, stamina, and agility—dance it at your own risk!

THE DOLLAR DANCE

Brides have the pleasure of dancing with many guests—and each one pins a dollar to her dress (or puts it in her purse). You can also include the groom in this one; have female guests and relatives dance with and pin money on him. The polka, with all its varied musical possibilities, is another staple at Polish receptions.

THE TANGO

Want to give your first dance a twist? Include this sensual South American stunner. Think about taking a few tango lessons, then clench that rose between your teeth and get out there!

"Born This Way," Lady Gaga

"Born to Be Wild," Steppenwolf

"The Boys of Summer," Don Henley

"Brick House," The Commodores

"Bring Me Some Water," Melissa Etheridge

"Can't Get Enough of Your Love, Babe," Barry White

"Cheers (Drink to That)," Rihanna

"Come On Eileen," Dexys Midnight Runners

"Conga," Miami Sound Machine

"Crazy," Britney Spears

"Crazy in Love," Snow Patrol

"Crazy Little Thing Called Love," Queen

"Dance to the Music," Sly & the Family Stone

"Dancing in the Street," Martha Reeves & The Vandellas or David
    Bowie and Mick Jagger

"Dancing Queen," ABBA

"December, 1963 (Oh, What a Night)," The Four Seasons

"Devil Went Down to Georgia," The Charlie Daniels Band

"Disco Inferno," Trammps

"Do You Love Me" The Contours

"Don't Bring Me Down," Electric Light Orchestra

"Don't Leave Me This Way," Thelma Houston

"Don't Rock the Jukebox," Alan Jackson

"Don't Stop Believin'," Journey

"Don't Stop the Music," Rihanna

"Don't Stop 'Til You Get Enough," Michael Jackson

"Don't You Want Me," The Human League

"Doo Wop (That Thing)," Lauryn Hill

"Down," Jay Sean

"Electric Avenue," Eddy Grant

"Enjoy the Silence," Depeche Mode

"Evacuate the Dance Floor," Cascada

"Every Little Thing She Does Is Magic," The Police

"Every Time We Touch," Cascada

"Everybody Have Fun Tonight," Wang Chung

"Fire," The Pointer Sisters or Bruce Springsteen

"Firework," Katy Perry

"Flashing Lights," Lupe Fiasco

"Freeze Frame," The J. Geils Band

"Friends in Low Places," Garth Brooks

"Funkytown," Lipps Inc.

silly dances

Come on, you know there's at least one of these that you secretly like! No, you don't have to play all these theme songs at your reception, but one or two may pull some people who otherwise wouldn't be caught dead on the dance floor right out there. Think of the pictures!

"Cha-Cha Slide,"
DJ Casper

"The Chicken Dance"

"Cupid Shuffle," Cupid

"The Electric Slide,"
Marcia Griffiths

"Gangnam Style," PSY

"Macarena (Bayside
Boys Mix)," Los del Rio

"YMCA," Village People

"The Gambler," Kenny Rogers

"Genie in a Bottle," Christina Aguilera

"Get Back," The Beatles

"Get Down on It," Kool & the Gang

"Get Down Tonight," KC & the Sunshine Band

"Gimme Some Lovin'," Steve Winwood

"Gonna Make You Sweat (Everybody Dance Now)," C&C Music Factory

"Good Lovin'," The Rascals

"Good Times," Chic

"Goody Two Shoes," Adam Ant

"Got to Be Real," Cheryl Lynn

"Groove Is in the Heart," Dee-Lite

"Heart of Glass," Blondie

"Heat Wave," Martha Reeves & The Vandellas

"Hold On," Wilson Phillips

"Holiday," Madonna

"Hot Hot Hot," Buster Poindexter

"Hungry Like the Wolf," Duran Duran

"The Hustle," Van McCoy & The Soul City Symphony

"I Feel Good," James Brown

"I Feel Love," Donna Summer

"I Got a Feeling," Black Eyed Peas

"I Knew the Bride (When She Used to Rock and Roll)," Nick Lowe

"I Melt with You," Modern English

"I Say a Little Prayer," Aretha Franklin or Dionne Warwick

"I Wanna Dance with Somebody," Whitney Houston

"I Want It That Way," Backstreet Boys

"I Will Survive," Gloria Gaynor

"If You Had My Love," Jennifer Lopez

"In Da Club," 50 Cent

"In the Mood," Glenn Miller Orchestra

"Into the Groove," Madonna

"It's the End of the World As We Know It (And I Feel Fine)," R.E.M.

"Jamming," Bob Marley

"Java Jive," Manhattan Transfer or The Ink Spots

"Jump, Jive, an' Wail," Louis Prima or Brian Setzer Orchestra

"Just Dance," Lady Gaga

"*La bamba*," Ritchie Valens

"Last Dance," Donna Summer

"Le Freak," Chic

"Let's Go Crazy," Prince and The Revolution

"Let's Spend the Night Together," The Rolling Stones

"Life in the Fast Lane," The Eagles

"Light My Fire," The Doors

"A Little Respect," Erasure

"Livin' *La vida loca*," Ricky Martin

"Livin' on a Prayer," Bon Jovi

"The Loco-Motion," Kylie Minogue or Grand Funk Railroad

"Love Shack," The B-52's

"Margaritaville," Jimmy Buffett

"Mickey," Toni Basil

"Missing," Everything But the Girl

"Mony Mony," Tommy James & The Shondells or Billy Idol

"Muskrat Ramble," Dukes of Dixieland or Harry Connick Jr.

"Mustang Sally," Rascals or The Commitments

"My Life Would Suck Without You," Kelly Clarkson

"Night Fever," The Bee Gees

"No Scrubs," TLC

"Now That We Found Love," Heavy D & the Boyz

"Old Time Rock 'n' Roll," Bob Seger & The Silver Bullet Band

"One Love," Bob Marley

"Party Rock Anthem," LMFAO

"Pink Cadillac," Bruce Springsteen or Southern Pacific

"Pop Muzik," M

"Pretty Woman," Roy Orbison

"Proud Mary," Creedence Clearwater Revival or Ike and Tina Turner

"Pump Up the Volume," M|A|R|R|S

"Raise Your Glass," Pink

"Red Red Wine," UB40

"Relax," Frankie Goes to Hollywood

"Respect," Aretha Franklin

"Rhythm Divine," Enrique Iglesias

"Rhythm of the Night," DeBarge

"Ring of Fire," Johnny Cash

"Rock Around the Clock," Bill Haley and The Comets

"Rockin' at Midnight," The Honeydrippers

"Rock This Town," Stray Cats

"Run-Around," Blues Traveler

"Save the Last Dance for Me," Tom Jones or The Drifters

"Say You'll Be There," Spice Girls

"September," Earth, Wind & Fire

"SexyBack," Justin Timberlake

"(Shake, Shake, Shake) Shake Your Booty," KC & the Sunshine Band
"Shake Your Groove Thing," Peaches & Herb
"Should I Stay or Should I Go," The Clash
"Shout," Otis Day & The Knights
"Single Ladies," Beyoncé
"Situation," Yaz
"So What," Pink
"Start Me Up," The Rolling Stones
"Stronger," Kanye West
"Sugarpie Honeybunch," Four Tops
"Superfreak," Rick James
"Superstition," Stevie Wonder
"Tainted Love," Soft Cell
"Take the 'A' Train," Duke Ellington or Cab Calloway
"Teenage Dream," Katy Perry
"Tequila," The Champs
"That's the Way (I Like It)," KC & The Sunshine Band
"This Kiss," Faith Hill
"Thriller," Michael Jackson
"Tik Tok," Ke$ha
"Try a Little Tenderness," Otis Redding
"Turn the Beat Around," Vicki Sue Robinson or Gloria Estefan
"Turn Your Love Around," George Benson
"The Twist," Chubby Checker
"Twist and Shout," The Beatles
"Twistin' the Night Away," Rod Stewart
"U Can't Touch This," MC Hammer
"Umbrella," Rihanna
"Upside Down," Diana Ross
"Venus," Bananarama or Shocking Blue
"Vogue," Madonna
"Volcano," Jimmy Buffett
"Wake Me Up Before You Go-Go," Wham
"Walking on Sunshine," Katrina & The Waves
"Wannabe," Spice Girls
"We Are Family," Sister Sledge
"We Got the Beat," The Go-Go's
"We Like to Party," Vengaboys
"West End Girls," Pet Shop Boys
"What I Like About You," The Romantics
"What Is Love," Haddaway

last-dance songs

Finish your night in style with one of these songs.

"American Pie," Don McLean

"Can't Take My Eyes Off You," Frankie Valli

"Closing Time," Semisonic

"Dancing Queen," ABBA

"Don't Stop Believin'," Journey

"Here Comes the Sun," The Beatles

"(I've Had) The Time of My Life," Bill Medley & Jennifer Warnes

"*Jai ho,*" A.R. Rahman

"Just Dance," Lady Gaga

"Last Dance," Donna Summer

"Let's Get It On," Marvin Gaye

"Livin' on a Prayer," Bon Jovi

"My Life Would Suck Without You," Kelly Clarkson

"New York, New York," Frank Sinatra

"Party Rock Anthem," LMFAO

"The Party's Over," Willie Nelson

"Piano Man," Billy Joel

"Raise Your Glass," Pink

"Save the Last Dance for Me," Michael Bublé

"Stand By Me," Ben E. King

"When I'm Sixty-Four," The Beatles

"Wonderful Tonight," Eric Clapton

"You Only Live Once," The Strokes

"You Shook Me All Night Long," AC/DC

"What You Need," INXS

"Where It's At," Beck

"Who Can It Be Now?" Men at Work

"Woodchopper's Ball," Duke Ellington or Benny Goodman

"Yeah," Usher

"(You Make Me Feel Like) A Natural Woman," Aretha Franklin

"You Only Live Once," The Strokes

"You Really Got Me," The Kinks or Van Halen

"You Sexy Thing," Hot Chocolate

"You Shook Me All Night Long," AC/DC

"You Should Be Dancing," The Bee Gees

"You Spin Me Round (Like a Record)," Dead or Alive

"(Your Love Keeps Lifting Me) Higher and Higher," Jackie Wilson

"You're the First, the Last, My Everything," Barry White

"You're the One That I Want," John Travolta and Olivia Newton-John

Notes _____

_____

_____

_____

_____

_____

_____

_____

_____

_____

_____

_____

_____

_____

_____

_____

_____

_____

_____

_____

_____

_____

_____

_____

_____

_____

_____

_____

_____

_____

_____

_____

6

speeches and toasts

Toasts from family and friends serve as entertainment and, well, an education. The toasting part of your reception is also a time for your guests to get to know you even better through the words of your closest friends and relatives. A room full of loved ones lifting a glass to you and speaking words of affection, recalling funny or touching stories about the two of you, offering compliments or telling jokes, and generally giving you a warm, fuzzy feeling (watch out for those tearjerker toasts!) can be one of the most memorable and meaningful parts of the party.

TALKING POINTS

- The best man usually serves as toastmaster. The maid of honor can take on this role—or serve as co-master—or she may simply toast the couple right after the best man does. Be sure your honor attendants know that they should lead the toasting.

- Traditionally the groom responds, thanking the best man and toasting his new wife; he may also offer his thanks and appreciation to their parents. These days, the bride also toasts her groom, or with him toasts and thanks their families and their guests.

- Your parents (especially if they are hosting the reception) and other relatives or friends may want to say something as well.

- Toasts usually happen once everyone has been seated and served drinks, but you may choose to wait to do it between courses—after the salad, for example. If either way sounds fine to you, leave it up to your honor attendants.

- Although your master of ceremonies (often the bandleader or DJ) may announce to guests that toasting is about to begin, we prefer it if the best man simply goes up to the microphone himself and begins. The traditional way to get people's attention is to clink a wineglass with a utensil. (Of course, guests also clink their glasses at a reception to get the newlyweds to kiss!)

- Make sure the microphone is tested before guests arrive in the reception area. It's nice to avoid all that screeching and awkwardness.

- Ask parents ahead of time whether they're interested in making a toast or speech; let them know you'd love it if they spoke, but they shouldn't feel obligated. Your father, with or without your mother, or even both sets of parents may also make a speech at the very beginning of the reception, before the "official" toasting begins, to welcome your guests. If they do so, they can still toast you as well at the appropriate time.

- At most Christian and Catholic weddings, a blessing is said before the meal is served; your officiant or a family elder may do the honors. At Jewish weddings, the bride's father says a traditional blessing over the challah bread, which is then torn into pieces and served to every table.

- If you're having a very large wedding, you might want to limit the toasting to just the honor attendants, your parents, and you two.

Save the stories and anecdotes for the more casual atmosphere of the rehearsal dinner or a postwedding brunch.

- That said, marathon toasting sessions have turned into a bit of a wedding trend. If you do want many people to be able to toast, maybe break it up into a few shorter sessions during the cocktail hour, during dinner, and during the cake cutting.

- If there are kids involved (for example, from a first marriage), offer them a chance to toast, or make sure to remember to toast them.

- Use the toasting ideas in this part as a starting point. You can integrate words into your own original speech ("As Voltaire said . . ."; "In the words of Willa Cather . . ."), giving them the significance you choose

---

ASK CARLEY

TOASTING DOS AND DON'TS

Are there any rules when it comes to toasting?

There are a few etiquette points to be aware of:

- When you're the one being toasted, stay seated, and don't raise your glass.

- If seated, stand when offering a toast, or "take the floor" at a microphone.

- The major players (honor attendants, newlyweds, parents) will probably want to prepare their speech or toast in advance, written out completely or at least in the form of notes. Emotions and nerves can get the best of you otherwise! You may even want to give it a practice run (or two).

- Keep it simple, and keep it personal. Don't try to be a performer if you're not, or use words you normally wouldn't use. Be yourself.

- Brevity is the soul of wit, remember? Even if you have a story to tell, don't use the long version.

- It's fine to drink from a glass of water or other beverage if you are not drinking alcohol; it's more polite than not drinking at all (although some say it's unlucky).

- To "finish" a toast, raise your glass, say the couple's names ("To Jacqueline and Ray"), and take a sip. Everyone else will follow your lead.

- If you're experiencing major stage fright as the bride or groom, remember: everyone in the room loves you! If you're an honor attendant and don't know everyone in the room, focus on the people you do know and love: the couple. Speak directly to them.

---

by relating them to the person or people you're toasting. The idea is to make everyone in the room feel the universal—and therefore personal—importance of the words.

TRADITIONAL AND CULTURAL TOASTS

May the road rise to meet you.
May the wind be always at your back,
the sun shine warm upon your face,
the rain fall soft upon your fields,
and until we meet again
may God hold you in the hollow of His hand.
—*Irish blessing*

Ten thousand things bright
Ten thousand miles, no dust
Water and sky one color
Houses shining along your road.
—*Chinese blessing*

Ka mau ki aha. ("May you never thirst again.")
—*Traditional Hawaiian wedding toast*

A toast to love and laughter,
and happily ever after.
—*Traditional toast*

May you grow old on one pillow.
—*Armenian blessing*

Where there is love there is no sin.
—*Montenegrin proverb*

When the husband drinks to the wife,
all would be well; when the wife drinks to the husband, all is.
—*English proverb*

May their joys be as bright as the morning, and their sorrows but shadows that fade in the sunlight of love.
—*Armenian blessing*

Happy the bride and bridegroom and thrice happy are they whose love grows stronger day by day and whose union remains undissolved until the last day.
—*African American blessing*

May your love be like the misty rain, gentle coming in but flooding the river.
—*African blessing*

May your love be as endless as your wedding rings.
—*Traditional blessing*

Marriage has teeth, and him bit very hot.
—*Jamaican proverb*

Mariel & Wide
APRIL 24
MIAMI, FLORIDA

Two maids of honor and two best men toasted Mariel and Wide at their wedding, but the most memorable moment came from one of the guys. Instead of a traditional speech, the best man read a list of things Wide needed to know now that he was a married man. This item on the list was particularly memorable: "Sleeping on the couch is not really a punishment, because men actually like it, but don't tell their wives."

May their joys be as deep as the ocean
And their misfortunes as light as the foam.
—*Armenian blessing*

Love is like a baby;
it needs to be treated gently.
—*Congolese proverb*

Ad multos annos—to many years!
—*Latin toast*

Deep love is stronger than life.
—*Jewish proverb*

Try to reason about love and you will lose your reason.
—*French proverb*

Love and eggs are best when they are fresh.
—*Russian proverb*

Let's drink to love, which is nothing—unless it's divided by two.
—*Irish blessing*

L'chaim! ("To life!")
—*Hebrew toast*

Here's to the bride and the groom!
May you have a happy honeymoon,
May you lead a happy life,
May you have a bunch of money soon,
And live without all strife.
—*Traditional toast*

Here's to the groom with bride so fair,
And here's to the bride with groom so rare!
—*Traditional toast*

Here's to the husband
And here's to the wife;
May they remain
Lovers for life.
—*Traditional toast*

May your joys be as sweet as spring flowers that grow.
As bright as a fire when winter winds blow,
As countless as leaves that float down in the fall,
As serene as the love that keeps watch over us all.
—*Old English blessing*

The heart that loves is always young.
—*Greek proverb*

Insomuch as love grows in you, so beauty grows. For love is
the beauty of the soul.
—*St. Augustine*

Let us toast the health of the bride;
Let us toast the health of the groom,
Let us toast the person that tied;
Let us toast every guest in the room.
—*Traditional toast*

BLESSINGS

Be present at our table, Lord.
Be here and everywhere adored.
Those mercies bless, and grant that we
May feast in Paradise with Thee.
—*John Cennick*

The Lord bless you and keep you!
The Lord let his face shine upon you,
and be gracious to you!
The Lord look upon you kindly and give you peace!
—*Numbers 6:24–26*

Bless, O Lord, this food to our use, and us to Thy service, and make
us ever needful of the needs of others, in Jesus's name. Amen.
—*Traditional Protestant grace*

Bless us, O Lord, and these Thy gifts which we have received out of Thy
bounty, through Christ Our Lord. Amen.
—*Traditional Catholic grace*

For what we are about to receive, the Lord make
us truly thankful, for Christ's sake. Amen.
What we are about to receive, may the Trinity
and the Unity bless. Amen.

—*Grace before meal*

Barukh atah Adonai Elohaynu melekh ha-olam ha-motzi lechem min ha-aretz. Blessed are You, Adonai our God, Source of the Universe, who
brings forth bread from the earth. Amen.

—*Traditional Jewish blessing over challah bread and wine (Ha-Motzi)*

All love should be simply stepping stones to the love of God. . . . Blessed
be His name for His great goodness and mercy.

—*Plato*

SHAKESPEAREAN TOASTS AND BLESSINGS

A flock of blessings light upon thy back.

—Romeo and Juliet, *Act III*

Fair thought and happy hours attend on you.

—The Merchant of Venice, *Act III*

Look down you gods,
And on this couple drop a blessed crown.

—The Tempest, *Act V*

I wish you all the joy you can wish.

—The Merchant of Venice, *Act III*

The best of happiness, honor, and fortunes keep, with you.

—Timon of Athens, *Act I*

God, the best maker of all marriages,
Combine your hearts in one.

—King Henry V, *Act V*

Love comforteth like sunshine after rain.
—*From "Venus and Adonis"*

Honor, riches, marriage-blessing,
Love continuance, and increasing,
Hourly joys be still upon you!
Juno sings her blessings on you.
—The Tempest, *Act IV*

TOASTS FROM MEMBERS OF THE WEDDING PARTY

We've organized the following toast ideas according to the wedding-party members we felt they would be appropriate for, but the list is not at all set in stone. Feel free to borrow from any section, no matter what your role in the wedding. The most important thing is that the words you choose to use contain the sentiment you want to convey. You'll want to speak personally for most of your toast, but these traditional toasts and sayings are wonderful to use when raising your glass when you come to a close, or as an introduction if you're trying to make a point about the couple's relationship that the quote embodies.

toasts from the best man

Those who have both true love and true friendship have received the highest gift God can offer.
—*Anonymous*

Shared joy is a double joy; shared sorrow is half a sorrow.
—*Swedish Proverb*

May you live as long as you want and want nothing as long as you live.
—*Traditional toast*

May you look back on the past with as much pleasure as you look forward to the future.
—*Irish toast*

Here's to health, peace, and prosperity;
May the flower of love never be nipped by the frost of disappointment;
Nor shadow of grief fall among a member of this circle.
—*Irish toast*

A health to you,
A wealth to you,
And the best that life can give to you.
May fortune still be kind to you.
And happiness be true to you,
And life be long and good to you,
Is the toast of all your friends to you.
—*Irish toast*

Cool breeze
Warm fire
Full moon
Easy chair
Empty plates
Soft words
Sweet songs
Tall tales
Short sips
Long life.
—*John Egerton*

Love is born with the pleasure of looking at each other, it is fed with the necessity of seeing each other, it is concluded with the impossibility of separation.
—*José Martí*

May the hinges of the friendship never rust, nor the wings of love lose a feather.
—*Allan Ramsay*

Marriage is the most natural state of man, and the state in which you will find solid happiness.
—*Benjamin Franklin*

I believe that love cannot be bought except with love, and he who has a good wife wears heaven in his hat.
—*John Steinbeck*

You have to walk carefully in the beginning of love; the running across fields into your lover's arms can only come later, when you're sure they won't laugh if you trip.
—*Jonathan Carroll*

Never do anything in the first year of your married life that you do not want to do for the rest of your life.
—*Naomi Fuller Worsley*

A man's growth is seen in the successive choirs of his friends.
—*Ralph Waldo Emerson*

Everything comes to us from others. To be is to belong to someone.
—*Jean-Paul Sartre*

There is no possession more valuable than a good and faithful friend.
—*Socrates*

Friendship is born at that moment when one person says to another: "What! You too? I thought I was the only one."
—*C. S. Lewis*

Marriage is our last, best chance to grow up.
—*Joseph Barth*

To keep your marriage brimming, with love in the wedding cup, whenever you're wrong, admit it; whenever you're right, shut up.
—*Ogden Nash*

As soon as you cannot keep anything from a woman, you love her.
—*Paul Géraldy*

The loving are the daring.
—*Bayard Taylor*

The most precious possession that ever comes to a man in this world is a woman's heart.
—*Josiah Gilbert Holland*

Who, being loved, is poor?
—*Oscar Wilde*

It is one of the blessings of old friends that you can afford to be stupid with them.
—*Ralph Waldo Emerson*

After all these years, I see that I was mistaken about Eve in the beginning; it is better to live outside the Garden with her than inside it without her.
—*Mark Twain*

I get by with a little help from my friends.
—*The Beatles*

In marriage do thou be wise: Prefer the person before money, virtue before beauty, the mind before the body; then thou hast a wife, a friend, a companion, a second self.
—*William Penn*

To the newlyweds: May "for better or worse" be far better than worse.
May the most you ever wish for be the least you ever receive.
May the saddest day of your future be no worse than the happiest day of your past.
—*Traditional toast*

toasts from the maid of honor

May there always be work for your hands to do.
May your purse always hold a coin or two.
May the sun always shine on your windowpane.
May a rainbow be certain to follow each rain.
May the hand of a friend always be near you.
May God fill your heart with gladness to cheer you.
—*Irish toast*

May your hands be forever clasped in friendship and your hearts joined forever in love.

—*Anonymous*

May the rocks in your field turn to gold.

—*Irish blessing*

Love is not finding someone to live with, it's finding someone you can't live without.

—*Rafael Ortiz*

All love is sweet, given or returned . . .
Those who inspire it most are fortunate . . .
But those who feel it most are happier still.

—*Percy Bysshe Shelley*

In a great romance, each person plays a part the other really likes.

—*Elizabeth Ashley*

The capacity to love is tied to being able to be awake, to being able to move out of yourself and be with someone else in a manner that is not about your desire to possess them, but to be with them, to be in union and communion.

—*Bell Hooks*

Love remains a secret even when spoken,
for only a true lover truly knows that he is loved.

—*Rabindranath Tagore*

Anyone can be passionate, but it takes real lovers to be silly.

—*Rose Franken*

We cannot really love anybody with whom we never laugh.

—*Agnes Repplier*

There is no more lovely, friendly, and charming relationship, communion, or company than a good marriage.

—*Martin Luther*

Let anniversaries come and let anniversaries go—but may your happiness continue on forever.
—*Anonymous*

Here's to marriage, that happy estate that resembles a pair of scissors: So joined that they cannot be separated, often moving in opposite directions, yet punishing anyone who comes between them.
—*Sidney Smith*

And this is my prayer: that your love may abound more and more in knowledge and depth of insight.
—*Philippians 1:9*

True friendship comes when silence between two people is comfortable.
—*Dave Tyson Gentry*

sing a song . . .

Not really, but do look to favorite song lyrics for inspiration in your toast. From old standards to totally contemporary tunes, there are definitely meaningful words to recall. A few examples:

"I can't help falling in love with you."
—*Elvis Presley*

"You are all I long for, all I worship and adore."
—*Frank Sinatra*

"Always, I want to be with you, to make believe with you, to live in harmony."
—*Erasure*

"You are my fire, my one desire."
—*Backstreet Boys*

"Your love is better than ice cream, better than anything else that I've found."
—*Sarah McLachlan*

"When the mountains crumble to the sea, it will still be you and me."
—*Led Zeppelin*

"I've been around enough to know that you're the one I want to go through time with."
—*Jim Croce*

"Here's my hand, reaching out for you; take it darling, it belongs to you."
—*Carlos Santana*

"You came along and stole my heart when you entered my life; ooh babe, you got what it takes, so I made you my wife."
—*Climax Blues Band*

"It's such a perfect day, I'm glad I spent it with you."
—*Lou Reed*

"Shut up and kiss me."
—*Mary Chapin Carpenter*

The time to be happy is now;
the place to be happy is here.
—*Robert G. Ingersoll*

Infatuation is when you think that he's as sexy as Robert Redford, as smart as Henry Kissinger, as noble as Ralph Nader, as funny as Woody Allen, and as athletic as Jimmy Connors. Love is when you realize that he's as sexy as Woody Allen, as smart as Jimmy Connors, as funny as Ralph Nader, as athletic as Henry Kissinger, and nothing like Robert Redford—but you'll take him anyway.
—*Judith Viorst*

Any time that is not spent on love is wasted.
—*Torquato Tasso*

Here's to the health of the happy pair;
May good luck follow them everywhere;
And may each day of wedded bliss
Be always as sweet and joyous as this.
—*Traditional toast*

For where the heart is, that is sure to be where your treasure is.
—*Matthew 6:21*

We never live so intensely as when we love strongly. We never realize ourselves so vividly as when we are in full glow of love for others.
—*Walter Rauschenbusch*

Never is true love blind, but rather brings an added light.
—*Phoebe Cary*

Keep love in your heart. A life without it is like a sunless garden when the flowers are dead. The consciousness of loving and being loved brings a warmth and richness to life that nothing else can bring.
—*Oscar Wilde*

Life is only life forevermore
Together wing to wing and oar to oar.
—*Robert Frost*

To love someone deeply gives you strength. Being loved by someone deeply gives you courage.

—*Lao Tzu*

Love is like a mirror. When you love another you become his mirror and he becomes yours. . . . And reflecting each other's love you see infinity.

—*Leo Buscaglia*

There is nothing more lovely in life than the union of two people whose love for one another has grown through the years from the small acorn of passion into a great rooted tree.

—*Vita Sackville-West*

Love, be true to her; Life, be dear to her;
Health, stay close to her; Joy, draw near to her;
Fortune, find what you can do for her,
Search your treasure-house through and through for her,
Follow her footsteps the wide world over—
And keep her husband always her lover.

—*Anna Lewis*

Love is like quicksilver in the hand. Leave the fingers open and it stays. Clutch it, and it darts away.

—*Dorothy Parker*

There is nothing I would not do for those who are really my friends. I have no notion of loving people by halves, it is not my nature.

—*Jane Austen*

True friends are like diamonds—bright, beautiful, valuable, and always in style.

—*Nicole Richie*

Sometimes you can't see yourself clearly until you see yourself through the eyes of others.

—*Ellen DeGeneres*

Every girl needs a good friend and a glass of wine.

—*LeAnn Rimes*

toasts from parents

When children find true love, parents find true joy.
Here's to your joy and ours, from this day forward.

—*Anonymous*

The way to Happiness:
Keep your heart free from hate,
Your mind from worry.
Live simply. Expect little. Give much.

—*Traditional saying*

Be ye kind to one another.

—*Ephesians 4:32*

Love one another and you will be happy. It's as simple and as difficult
as that.

—*Michael Leunig*

A good marriage is at least 80 percent good luck in finding the right
person at the right time. The rest is trust.

—*Nanette Newman*

If you are considering marriage, ask yourself one question: Will I still
enjoy talking with her when I'm old?

—*Friedrich Nietzsche*

Chains do not hold a marriage together. It is threads, hundreds of tiny
threads which sew people together through the years. That is what
makes a marriage last.

—*Simone Signoret*

Success in marriage depends on being able, when you get over being in
love, to really love. . . . You never know anyone until you marry them.

—*Eleanor Roosevelt*

The great secret of a successful marriage is to treat all disasters as
incidents and none of the incidents as disasters.

—*Sir Harold Nicolson*

Love and work are the cornerstones of our humanness.

—*Sigmund Freud*

Love does not dominate; it cultivates.
—*Johann Wolfgang von Goethe*

Love is blind—marriage is the eye-opener.
—*Pauline Thomason*

The first duty of love is to listen.
—*Paul Tillich*

There is no remedy for love but to love more.
—*Henry David Thoreau*

Immature love says: "I love you because I need you." Mature love says: "I need you because I love you."
—*Erich Fromm*

It is wrong to think that love comes from long companionship and persevering courtship. Love is the offspring of spiritual affinity, and unless that affinity is created in a moment, it will not be created for years or even generations.
—*Kahlil Gibran*

Love is everything it's cracked up to be. That's why people are so cynical about it. It really is worth fighting for, being brave for, risking everything for. And the trouble is, if you don't risk anything, you risk even more.
—*Erica Jong*

Marriage is an edifice that must be rebuilt every day.
—*André Maurois*

The story of a love is not important—what is important is that one is capable of love. It is perhaps the only glimpse we are permitted of eternity.
—*Helen Hayes*

The man or woman you really love will never grow old to you. Through the wrinkles of time, through the bowed frame of years, you will always see the dear face and feel the warm heart union of your eternal love.
—*Alfred A. Montapert*

You will find as you look back upon your life that the moments when you have truly lived are the moments when you have done things in the spirit of love.

—*Henry Drummond*

Everyone admits that love is wonderful and necessary, yet no one agrees on just what it is.

—*Diane Ackerman*

The only way of full knowledge lies in the act of love; this act transcends thought, it transcends words. It is the daring plunge into the experience of union. To love somebody is not just a strong feeling—it is a decision, it is a judgment, it is a promise.

—*Erich Fromm*

Whatever you do, love those who love you.

—*Voltaire*

A successful marriage requires falling in love many times, always with the same person.

—*Mignon McLaughlin*

When angry, count to a hundred.

—*Mark Twain*

Age does not protect you from love, but love to some extent protects you from age.

—*Jeanne Moreau*

Love consists in this: That two solitudes protect and touch and greet each other.

—*Rainer Maria Rilke*

A generation of children on the children of your children.

—*Irish blessing*

Grandchildren are the crown of old men,
And the glory of sons is their fathers.

—*Proverbs 17:6*

toasting with taste

Champagne is always perfect for toasting, but you can add a more cultural touch by clinking with beer, whiskey, or shots of vodka, rum, sake, or tequila. Just ask your waitstaff to pass your choice around right before the toast.

You don't marry one person; you marry three—the person you think they are, the person they are, and the person they are going to become as the result of being married to you.
—*Richard J. Needham*

May you have enough happiness to keep you sweet;
enough trials to keep you strong;
enough sorrow to keep you human;
enough hope to keep you happy;
enough failure to keep you humble;
enough success to keep you eager;
enough friends to give you comfort;
enough faith and courage in yourself, your business, and your country to
    banish depression;
enough wealth to meet your needs;
enough determination to make each day a better day than yesterday.
—*Traditional blessing*
[Feel free to make up your own additional points.]

The more that you love one another, the closer you will come to God.
—*Traditional saying*

Without understanding, your love is not true love. You must look deeply in order to see and understand the needs, aspirations, and suffering of the one you love.
—*Thich Nhat Hanh*

A family starts with a young man falling in love with a girl. No superior alternative has been found.
—*Winston Churchill*

Coming together is a beginning;
Keeping together is progress;
Working together is success.
—*Henry Ford*

Never go to bed angry. Stay up and fight.
—*Phyllis Diller*

When in doubt, tell the truth.
—*Mark Twain*

toasting templates

Do you work better with some structure?
Here are a few clever ways to think about your toast while you're writing it:

TOP 10 LIST

For example, "Top ten reasons why it's great that Brian is marrying Sara."

FAMILIAR VERSE

Write your toast based on slightly singsongy words that everyone recognizes, like "'Twas the Night Before Christmas" (make it "'Twas the Night Before the Wedding," or "'Twas the Night Before the Proposal," perhaps).

THE ALPHABET

Talk about the bride's and/or groom's attributes by listing them based on the letters of each person's name. For example, Scott might be Secure, Courageous, Off-center, Tender, and Talented. Elaborate on each one.

ANALOGY OR METAPHOR

Use an overriding theme to shape your speech and make your point (for example, "Marriage is like climbing a mountain").

Don't smother each other. No one can grow in shade.

—*Leo Buscaglia*

There is no secret to a long marriage—it's hard work. . . . It's serious business, and certainly not for cowards.

—*Ossie Davis*

Be of love (a little) more careful than of anything.

—*E. E. Cummings*

The secret of health, happiness, and long life: If you simply learn how to accept and express love, you will live longer . . . be happier . . . grow healthier. For love is a powerful force.

—*Alfred A. Montapert*

May I wish for you the knowledge . . . that marriages do not Take Place, they are made by hand; that there is always an element of discipline involved; that however perfect the honeymoon, the time will come, however brief it is, when you will wish she would fall downstairs and break a leg. This goes for her, too. But the mood will pass, if you give it time.

—*Raymond Chandler*

You can't be that kid standing at the top of the waterslide, overthinking it. You have to go down the chute.
—*Tina Fey*

toasts from siblings and/or adult children

Love does not consist in gazing at each other, but in looking outward together in the same direction.
—*Antoine de Saint-Exupéry*

May you have warm words on a cold evening,
A full moon on a dark night,
And the road downhill all the way to your door.
—*Irish blessing*

There is no surprise more magical than the surprise of being loved. It is God's finger on man's shoulder.
—*Charles Morgan*

Love is not a matter of counting the years, it is making the years count. Love is the master key that opens the gates of happiness.
—*Oliver Wendell Holmes*

To get the full value of a joy you must have somebody to divide it with.
—*Mark Twain*

If it is your time, love will track you down like a cruise missile.
—*Lynda Barry*

When you love someone, all your saved-up wishes start coming out.
—*Elizabeth Bowen*

Love is love's reward.
—*John Dryden*

Only the complete person can love.
—*Confucius*

When love and skill work together, expect a masterpiece.
—*John Ruskin*

Our affections are our life. We live by them; they supply our warmth.
—*Anonymous*

To your coming anniversaries—may they be outnumbered only by your coming pleasures.
—*Anonymous*

What greater thing is there for two human souls than to feel that they are joined . . . to strengthen each other . . . to be at one with each other in silent unspeakable memories.
—*George Eliot*

May your hands be forever clasped in friendship and your hearts joined forever in love.
—*Traditional blessing*

A happy marriage perhaps represents the ideal of human relationship—a setting in which each partner, while acknowledging the need of the other, feels free to be what he or she by nature is: a relationship in which instinct as well as intellect can find expression; in which giving and taking are equal; in which each accepts the other.
—*Anthony Storr*

A life lived in love will never be dull.
—*Leo Buscaglia*

May you be poor in misfortune
Rich in blessings
Slow to make enemies
And quick to make friends.
But rich or poor, quick or slow,
May you know nothing but happiness
From this day forward.
—*Traditional blessing*

Though weary, love is not tired;
Though pressed, it is not straitened;
Though alarmed, it is not confounded.
Love securely passes through all.
—*Thomas à Kempis*

Where there is great love, there are always miracles.
—*Willa Cather*

Only once in your life, I truly believe, you find someone who can completely turn your world around.
—*Bob Marley*

Love recognizes no barriers. It jumps hurdles, leaps fences, penetrates walls to arrive at its destination full of hope.
—*Maya Angelou*

toasts from partner to partner

If ever two were one, then surely we.
If ever man were lov'd by wife, then thee;
If ever wife was happy in a man,
Compare with me, ye women, if you can.
I prize thy love more than whole mines of gold,
Or all the riches that the East doth hold.
My love is such that rivers cannot quench,
Nor ought but love from thee, give recompense.
Thy love is such I can no way repay,
The heavens reward thee manifold, I pray.
Then while we live, in love let's so persevere
That when we live no more, we may live ever.
—*Anne Bradstreet*

If I know what love is, it is because of you.
—*Hermann Hesse*

Yet everything that touches us, me and you,
takes us together like a violin's bow,
which draws one voice out of two separate strings.
Upon what instrument are we two spanned?
And what musician holds us in his hand?
Oh, sweetest song.
—*Rainer Maria Rilke*

The minute I heard my first love story
I started looking for you, not knowing
how blind that was.
Lovers don't finally meet somewhere.
They're in each other all along.
—*Rumi*

Because I love you truly,
Because you love me, too,
My very greatest happiness
Is sharing life with you.
—*Minna Thomas Antrim*

My bounty is as boundless as the sea,
My love as deep; the more I give to thee,
The more I have, for both are infinite.
—*William Shakespeare*

Love is what you've been through with somebody.
—*James Thurber*

May we love as long as we live,
and live as long as we love.
—*Anonymous*

To love a person means to agree to grow old with him.
—*Albert Camus*

Your words dispel all of the care in the world and make me happy. . . .
They are as necessary to me now as sunlight and air. . . . Your words are
my food, your breath my wine—you are everything to me.
—*Sarah Bernhardt*

Your life and my life flow into each other as wave flows into wave, and
unless there is peace and joy and freedom for you, there can be no real
peace or joy or freedom for me. To see reality—not as we expect it to
be but as it is—is to see that unless we live for each other and in and
through each other, we do not really live very satisfactorily; that there
can really be life only where there really is, in just this sense, love.
—*Frederick Buechner*

With one glance
I loved you
With a thousand hearts.

—*Mihri Hatun*

Come the wild weather,
come sleet or come snow,
We will stand by each other,
however it blow.

—*Simon Dach*

Our kindred spirits love and are loved like the sun and moon shining in
together from all sides.

—*Turkish saying*

My sweetheart
a long time
I have been waiting for you
to come over
where I am.

—*Chippewa song*

My fellow, my companion, held most dear,
My soul, my other self, my inward friend.

—*Mary Sidney Herbert*

Love me, sweet, with all thou art,
Feeling, thinking, seeing,—
Love me in the lightest part,
Love me in full being.

—*Elizabeth Barrett Browning*

I am not sure that Earth is round
Nor that the sky is really blue.
The tale of why the apples fall
May or may not be true.
I do not know what makes the tides
Nor what tomorrow's world may do,
But I have certainty enough,
For I am sure of you.

—*Amelia Josephine Burr*

His mouth is sweetness itself;
he is all delight.
Such is my lover, and such my friend,
O daughters of Jerusalem.

—*Song of Solomon*

We are custodians, keeper of each other's hearts and secrets. We treasure them with tenderness and fidelity. There is always risk when one is dealing with priceless treasures. But we . . . prefer to take that risk.

—*Lionel A. Whiston*

Drink to me only with thine eyes,
And I will pledge with mine;
Or leave a kiss within the cup,
And I'll not look for wine.

—*Ben Jonson*

what did you just say?

Before you write your toasts, read this.

WHAT'S TOASTING-APPROPRIATE:

- Beginning by saying you are honored to be here to share the wedding day with the couple.

- Talking casually about your relationship with the bride and/or groom (what it is, when you met) and relating one or two quick anecdotes.

- Pointing out what's special about their relationship and why you think they're perfect for each other.

- Offering gentle advice about marriage or love from your own experience.

WHAT'S NOT APPROPRIATE:

- Dwelling on potentially touchy subjects, like a difference in religion or race, or an ex-spouse.

- Apologizing for being a bad speaker, or saying you didn't really want to speak.

- Talking too much about the bride's or groom's past conquests (you may do so in a short-and-sweet, harmless way).

- Being cryptic (don't tell stories that only the bride and groom will understand; you'll lose your audience).

- Talking for too long—longer than five minutes.

- Fidgeting or clearing your throat (if you feel dry, keep a glass of water close by and take a quick sip before you begin talking).

Grow old along with me!
The best is yet to be.
—*Robert Browning*

Wherever I roam, whatever realms I see,
My heart untravelled fondly returns to thee.
—*Oliver Goldsmith*

Just to see her was to love her,
Love but her, and love forever.
—*Robert Burns*

When the heart is full, the tongue cannot speak.
—*Scottish proverb*

You are all-beautiful, my beloved,
and there is no blemish in you.
—*Song of Solomon*

I have spread my dreams under your feet;
Tread softly, because you tread on my dreams.
—*William Butler Yeats*

The hours I spend with you I look upon as sort of a perfumed garden, a
dim twilight, and a fountain singing to it . . . you and you alone make me
feel that I am alive. . . . Other men it is said have seen angels, but I have
seen thee, and thou art enough.
—*George Moore*

If I were to lose everything I had worked for in life all at once . . . As long
as I still had you I would feel as if I were the richest man in the world.
—*Michael Wheeler*

Doubt thou that the stars are fire;
Doubt that the sun doth move;
Doubt truth to be a liar;
But never doubt I love.
—*William Shakespeare*

the last word

Here are toasting words from around the world.
All translate to "To your health," unless otherwise noted.

Cheers!
 —*English, Australian*

Á votre santé!
 —*French*

Salud!
 —*Spanish, Mexican, Latin American*

Salud, pesetas, y amor . . . y tiempo para gozarlos!
("Health, money, and love . . . and time to enjoy them!")
 —*Spanish*

Salute! or *Cin Cin!* ("All things good for you!")
 —*Italian*

Prosit!
 —*Austrian, German*

Za vashe zdorovia!
 —*Russian*

Kanpai! ("Bottoms up/Dry glass!") or *Banzai!*
("Our last farewell!")
 —*Japanese*

Kanpei! ("Dry glass!")
 —*Chinese*

Mazel tov! ("Congratulations!")
 —*Jewish*

Sláinte!
 —*Scottish/Gaelic*

Stin yeia sou! or *Opa!* ("Hooray!")
 —*Greek*

Chai yo!
 —*Thai*

Chu kha ham ni da! ("Congratulations!")
 —*Korean*

Skål!
 —*Scandinavian*

Kou ola kino! or *Hauoli maoli oe!* ("To your happiness!")
 —*Hawaiian*

Aap ki sehat ke liye!
 —*Indian (Hindu)*

I have spread no snares today;
I am caught in my love of you.
—*Egyptian saying*

She walks in Beauty, like the night
Of cloudless climes and starry skies;
And all that's best of dark and bright
Meet in her aspect and her eyes:
Thus mellowed to that tender light
Which Heaven to gaudy day denies.
—*Lord Byron*

I love you,
Not only for what you are,
But for what I am
When I am with you.
I love you,
Not only for what
You have made of yourself
But for what you are making of me.
—*Roy Crots*

Soft lips, can I tempt you to an eternity of kissing?
—*Ben Jonson*

Here is to loving, to romance, to us.
May we travel together through time.
We alone count as none, but together we're one.
For our partnership puts love to rhyme.
—*Irish blessing*

Thou art the star that guides me
Along life's changing sea;
And whatever fate betides me,
This heart still turns to thee.
—*George P. Morris*

Each shining light about us
Has its own peculiar grace,
But every light of heaven
Is in my darling's face.
—*John Hay*

Love not me for comely grace
For my pleasing eye or face,
Nor for any outward part,
No, nor for my constant heart;
For those may fail or turn to ill,
So thou and I shall sever;
Keep therefore a true woman's eye,
And love me still, but know not why.
So hast thou the same reason still
To dote upon me ever.
—*Anonymous*

Give me a kiss, and to that kiss a score;
Then to that twenty, add a hundred more;
A thousand to that hundred; so kiss on,
To make that thousand up a million;
Treble that million, and when that is done,
Let's kiss afresh, as when we first begun.
—*Robert Herrick*

It warms me, it charms me,
To mention but her name,
It heats me, it beats me,
And sets me heart on flame.
—*Robert Burns*

Thou hast no faults, or I no faults can spy;
Thou art all beauty, or all blindness I.
—*Anonymous*

Here's to my mother-in-law's daughter,
Here's to her father-in-law's son;
And here's to the vows we've just taken,
And the life we've just begun.
—*Traditional toast*

But here's the joy; my friend and I are one . . .
Then she loves but me alone!
—*William Shakespeare*

To my wife,
My bride and joy.
—*Anonymous*

Here's to you who halves my sorrows and doubles my joys.
—*Anonymous*

I'm here today because I refused to be unhappy. I took a chance.
—*Wanda Sykes*

The future for me is already a thing of the past
You were my first love and you will be my last
—*Bob Dylan*

prewedding party toasting

At an engagement party, the father of the bride toasts the couple and formally announces their engagement to those gathered. Other relatives and friends may say something, as well.

AT A SHOWER

A toast is not traditionally part of this party, but close relatives and friends should feel free to formally share their good wishes for you in front of the other guests. A popular activity at a bridal shower is for the guests to tell funny or touching stories or to share marriage wisdom with the bride.

AT BACHELOR/BACHELORETTE PARTIES

This is where the "raunchier" toasts can be offered, or where the bride's or groom's past romantic life can be mentioned or poked harmless fun at by attendants and friends. Just don't go too far if parents are on hand!

AT A REHEARSAL DINNER

If you're inviting out-of-town guests and this event will be rather large, it's a great opportunity for people to toast the couple. The hosts of the party—traditionally the groom's parents—might begin by welcoming the guests and thanking them for traveling to the wedding. Then the best man can start the toasting, and things progress quite similarly to how they will at the wedding. If you will invite only your immediate families and the wedding party to the rehearsal dinner, you can eliminate the toasting or simply do it very casually.

When you realize you want to spend the rest of your life with somebody, you want the rest of your life to start as soon as possible.
—When Harry Met Sally

Every little look inside your eyes
Is all it takes to make me realize
We can last forever.
—Chicago

I hope you don't mind that I put down in words
How wonderful life is while you're in the world.
—Elton John

What better way could anything end? Hand in hand, with my friend.
—The Muppets

toasts from couple to parents

All that I am or hope to be, I owe to my angel mother.
—*Abraham Lincoln*

Oh, the love of a mother, love which none can forget.
—*Victor Hugo*

A mother is the truest friend we have.
—*Washington Irving*

God could not be everywhere, so he made mothers.
—*Proverb*

A father is someone you look up to no matter how tall you grow.
—*Anonymous*

Directly after God in heaven comes Papa.
—*Wolfgang Amadeus Mozart*

My father has given me the greatest treasure a father can give—a piece of himself.
—*Suzanne Chazin*

I'm lucky I'm in love with my best friend,
Lucky to have been where I have been,
Lucky to be coming home again.
—*Jason Mraz*

toasts from couple to guests

May the friends of our youth be the companions of our old age.
—*Traditional toast*

Among those whom I like, I can find no common denominator, but among those whom I love, I can; all of them make me laugh.
—*W. H. Auden*

Here's to Eternity—may we spend it in as good company as this night finds us.
—*Traditional toast*

It is around the table that friends understand best the warmth of being together.
—*Italian proverb*

Happiness consists not in the multitude of friends but in their worth and choice.
—*Ben Jonson*

May our house always be too small to hold all our friends.
—*Myrtle Reed*

To friendship: The only cement that will hold the world together.
—*Traditional toast*

Absent friends—though out of sight we recognize them with our glasses.
—*Anonymous toast*

SOURCE BIOGRAPHIES

Here are a few words about each of the writers featured in the readings section.

Dante Alighieri (1265–1321) was an Italian poet of the Middle Ages who is well known as the author of the *Divine Comedy*, an epic poem divided into three parts (*Inferno*, *Purgatorio*, and *Paradiso*) that is one of the great masterpieces of world literature.

Yehuda Amichai (1924–2000) immigrated to Israel from Germany in 1936 and is considered Israel's most important poet. He has published eleven volumes of poetry in Hebrew, two novels, and a book of short stories, and his work has been translated into more than thirty languages.

Maya Angelou (1928–) began her prolific writing career as a performer and playwright. Her repertoire grew to include her acclaimed first book, *I Know Why the Caged Bird Sings* (1970), screenwriting, and poetry. She was awarded the Presidential Medal of Arts in 2000, the Lincoln Medal in 2008, and the Presidential Medal of Freedom in 2011 and has won three Grammy Awards.

Andrew Boyd (1963–) is a humorous author, satirist, activist. speaker, and self-described prankster. He lives in New York.

Charlotte Brontë (1816–1855) was an English novelist and poet writing during the Victorian era. She published four novels, the most famous of which is *Jane Eyre*.

Emily Brontë (1818–1848), Charlotte's slightly younger sister (they had another writer sibling, Anne), wrote poetry in addition to her intense, passionate, and much-loved novel *Wuthering Heights*. All her work displays her preoccupation with love and death.

Elizabeth Barrett Browning (1806–1861) was married to the poet Robert Browning, and her feelings for him inspired her love poetry. Her *Sonnets from the Portuguese* details her love affair with Robert.

Robert Burns (1759–1796) was a Scottish poet and lyricist known for his satire and wit. He set many verses to old Scottish tunes.

Leo Buscaglia (1924–1998) was a renowned lecturer and professor at the University of Southern California. Author of such books as *Living, Loving and Learning* and *Born for Love,* he was a tireless advocate of the power of love, promoting the creation of loving relationships and the pursuit of happiness.

Leonard Cohen (1934–) is a Canadian singer-songwriter who was named among the "highest and most influential echelon of songwriters" when he was inducted into the Rock and Roll Hall of Fame in 2008. His most well-known songs include "Hallelujah," "Suzanne," and "Famous Blue Raincoat."

Billy Collins (1941–) served as America's poet laureate from 2001 to 2003 and has been called "the most popular poet in America" by the *New York Times.* His bestselling collections of poetry include *Picnic, Lightning,* and *Sailing Alone Around the Room.*

E. E. Cummings (1894–1962) is best known for his all-lowercase poetic style and the fun he had with punctuation and spacing. He wrote many deeply emotional poems filled with sensual imagery and often touched with gentle humor.

Michael Drayton (1563–1631) was an Elizabethan poet who wrote much about love and heroism. He is known for the nationalistic ode "Ballad of Agincourt" and the end-of-love poem "Since There's No Help."

Carol Ann Duffy (1955–), who hails from Scotland, became Britain's first female poet laureate in 2009. Her poem "Rings" was written for the royal wedding of Prince William and Kate Middleton in 2011.

Paul Laurence Dunbar (1872–1906) was America's first nationally known African American poet. The son of former slaves, Dunbar published short stories, novels, and a play in addition to his poetry. Maya Angelou used a line from his work as the title of her book *I Know Why the Caged Bird Sings.*

Bob Dylan (1941–) is one of the most celebrated and honored figures in popular music. His socially charged songs like "Blowin' in the Wind" and "The Times They Are A-Changin'" became anthems of the 1960s, and he has continued to influence musicians over the decades since then. He was inducted into the Rock and Roll Hall of Fame in 1986.

Ralph Waldo Emerson (1803–1882) was an American philosopher, essayist, lecturer, and poet. He was a Unitarian minister for a time before he became interested in transcendentalism, which drew upon the teachings of Hinduism, among other philosophies.

Arthur Davison Ficke (1883–1945) was an American poet. In 1916 he, along with two friends, concocted a fanciful group of experimental poets called the Spectric school. In addition to his poetry, Ficke's interpretation of Japanese painting enjoyed an international reputation.

Robert Frost (1874–1963) was an acclaimed American poet. He was born in San Francisco, but spent most of his life living in New England and Great Britain. Frost won four Pulitzer Prizes for his poetry, and his most well-known poems include "Fire and Ice," "The Road Not Taken" and "Nothing Gold Can Stay."

Deborah Garrison (1965–) published her first volume of poetry, *A Working Girl Can't Win*, in 1998 and followed it ten years later with *The Second Child*, which deals with themes of motherhood in marriage. In addition to writing poetry, Garrison is an editor at Pantheon Books.

Kahlil Gibran (1883–1931) was a Lebanese poet and novelist who wrote in both English and Arabic; he lived for a time in New York. Fusing elements of Eastern and Western mysticism, his 1923 book *The Prophet* is well known and often read at weddings.

Nikki Giovanni (1943–) is an African American poet, writer, activist, and educator. She is the author of the book *Racism 101* and more than fourteen volumes of poetry.

Rob Hardy (1964–) is an editor, teacher, and writer whose poetry has appeared in *The Red Cedar Review, Rattle,* and *The Comstock Review,* among other publications. He has contributed to Garrson Keillor's *The Writer's Almanac* and writes a blog called *Rough Draft.* He lives in Northfield, Minnesota.

Seamus Heaney (1939–) is an Irish poet who writes frequently about his homeland—from his early naturalist work to contemporary Ireland, and most recently about his own exile. He won the Nobel Prize in Literature in 1995.

Jane Hirshfield (1953–) once studied Zen Buddhism and says she has been influenced by both Eastern and Western traditions. In addition to penning several volumes of verse, she has translated and anthologized the works of many early women poets.

Brendan Kennelly (1936–) is nearly as well-known in his native Ireland as his countryman Bono, whom he counts as a friend. The author of more than twenty books of poetry, as well as novels, plays, and criticism, he has taught at Trinity College in Dublin for more than thirty years.

Christopher Marlowe (1564–1593) wrote poetry and plays; it was said he was often imitated by Shakespeare early on. One controversial speculation holds that Marlowe faked an early death and took up a new identity—as William Shakespeare! One of his most famous works is his play *Doctor Faustus.*

Janet Miles's poem "Two Trees" is included in the book *Images of Women in Transition* (Saint Mary's Press, 1991).

John Milton (1608–1674) was an English writer famous for his incredible epic poem *Paradise Lost,* excerpted here, as well as *Paradise Regained.* Earlier in his life, he had written many controversial religious pamphlets.

Thomas Moore (1779–1852) was an Irish poet and patriot probably best known for his *Irish Melodies,* a group of lyrics set to music (one of which is the poem published here, "Believe Me, If All Those Endearing Young Charms"). He was a friend of Lord Byron and published a notable biography of him.

William Morris (1834–1896) was an English writer and poet who early on became a member of painter-poet Dante Gabriel Rossetti's Pre-Raphaelite movement. He wrote many historical epic poems, and eventually became involved in the socialist movement, which he wrote about widely.

Ogden Nash (1902–1971) was an American poet and humorist who wrote a wide range of highly comical, often absurd, and always quotable light verse.

Pablo Neruda (1904–1973) was a Chilean poet, diplomat, and communist leader who wrote surreal, highly personal, and sensual verse. He won the Nobel Prize in Literature in 1971, and he was rendered as a likable, romantic character in the 1995 movie *Il Postino*.

Oriah (1954–), also known as Oriah Mountain Dreamer, is a Canadian author. Her books, which include *The Invitation, The Dance, and The Call*, incorporate prose, poetry, and nonfiction stories focused on spirituality.

Kenneth Patchen (1911–1972) was an American poet and novelist known for his free-form verse and wide-ranging subject matter, from satire to metaphysical love poetry. He often illustrated his books with his own drawings.

Marge Piercy (1936–) is an American poet, novelist, and social activist and is one of the bestselling poets in the United States today. Her work often addresses issues of Judaism, feminism, and ecology.

Kenneth Rexroth (1905–1982) was an American poet, critic, and translator associated with the Beat writers and poets in San Francisco. He translated much Asian poetry, including "Married Love" by Kuan Tao-shêng, which appears in this book. He also wrote a book of verse plays and several books of essays.

Rainer Maria Rilke (1875–1926) was born in Prague and lived and wrote his passionate, insightful poetry and prose in Munich. The most famous are probably *Letters to a Young Poet* and the *Duino Elegies*. Stephen Mitchell has translated much of Rilke's work.

Tom Robbins (1936–) made his mark as a chronicler of the counterculture and is known for offbeat novels that combine wildly inventive plots with a subversive social message, including *Even Cowgirls Get the Blues* and *Still Life with Woodpecker*. He lives in Washington State.

Christina Rossetti (1830–1894), a British poet, was seen by many as an early feminist, constantly trying to reconcile her own conflicting views about religion, ambition, familial obligation, and Victorian ideals of what a woman should be. She wrote introspective, emotional poetry about love. Her brother Dante Gabriel Rossetti was also a poet.

Rumi (1207–1273) was a Persian poet and mystic. His major work is the *Mathnawi*, a vast work of spiritual teaching in incredibly beautiful and lyric stories and poetry. It is one of the enduring treasures of the Persian-speaking world. He wrote the poem "This Marriage" for his son's wedding.

Antoine de Saint-Exupéry (1900–1944) was a French writer, poet, and aviator whose writings have been translated into hundreds of languages. *The Little Prince* (1943) still sells 135,000 copies a year in the United States, some seventy years after it was written.

Sappho was born on the island of Lesbos sometime between 630 and 612 BCE and earned a reputation as one of the greatest lyric poets of antiquity. Her themes deal with love and passion for both men and women—the word "sapphic" is derived from her name.

William Shakespeare (1564–1616) is widely regarded as the greatest playwright in the English language. Among his many histories, comedies, and tragedies, plays like *Romeo and Juliet*, *Hamlet*, *King Lear*, *Othello*, *Macbeth*, and *A Midsummer Night's Dream* are some of the most read and well known. He also wrote poetry, including 154 sonnets (several of which are included in this book); the sonnets are by far his most important nondramatic verse.

Sir Philip Sidney (1554–1586) was one of the most important and innovative figures of the sixteenth-century English Renaissance, along with Shakespeare and Edmund Spenser. His best-known work is the sonnet sequence *Astrophel and Stella*.

Kuan Tao-shêng (1262–1319), also known as Madame Kuan, was the wife of Chao-Meng-Fu, a noted Chinese painter and calligrapher, Besides being a poet, she also painted and did calligraphy herself.

Sara Teasdale (1884–1933) was an American poet who wrote lyrical and highly personal works. Her book *Love Songs* won the Pulitzer Prize for Poetry in 1918. She was quite reclusive and, unfortunately, died by her own hand at the age of forty-eight.

Lao Tzu (sixth century BCE), a philosopher and poet of ancient china, wrote the *Tao Te Ching* and is considered the founder of Taoism. He was supposedly appointed head librarian of the imperial archives at Luoyang, where he immersed himself in the study of history, philosophy, and literature. Confucius visited with him and was in awe of his intellect. When Lao Tzu decided to leave civilization behind and departed Luoyang, a guard at the gate asked him to write down his thoughts on the Tao for posterity. Lao Tzu agreed, and the work came to be known as the *Tao Te Ching*.

Walt Whitman (1819–1892) was the most influential American poet of his time. He worked as a journalist in and around New York City before turning to poetry. His first effort was the daring poetry collection *Leaves of Grass*.

William Carlos Williams (1883–1963) was a pioneer of American poetry, known for his experimentation with meter and the way lines are broken. His most well-known anthologies of poetry include *Spring and All*, *Paterson*, and *Imaginations*.

RESOURCES

officiants/vows

Barbara Ann Michaels, multifaith wedding officiant
ArtfulLove.Blogspot.com

Reverend Gary Rozman, nondenominational minister
RevRoz.com

Chris Robinson, nondenominational minister
OfficiantGuy.com

Bill Swetmon, nondenominational minister
214-804-6591

Joyce Gioia, multifaith clergywoman
MultifaithWeddings.com

Joan Hawxhurst, founding editor of Dovetail Publishing, author
of *Interfaith Wedding Ceremonies: Samples and Sources* (Dovetail
Publishing, 1996)
joan@hawxhurst@kzoo.edu

The Reverends Irwin and Florence Schnurman, interfaith ministers
631-345-3606; weddings@alphamedia.net

Dr. Tino Ballesteros, executive pastor, Yosemite Church

PERMISSIONS

I gratefully acknowledge the following sources, which are included in this book. They are listed alphabetically by author's last name.

Yehuda Amichai: "I Sat in the Happiness" from *Yehuda Amichai: A Life of Poetry 1948–1994* by Yehuda Amichai. Translated by Benjamin and Barbara Harshav. Copyright © 1994 by HarperCollins Publishers, Inc. Hebrew-language version copyright © 1994 by Yehuda Amichai. Reprinted by permission of HarperCollins Publishers.

Andrew Boyd: "Loving the Wrong Person" from *Daily Afflictions: The Agony of Being Connected to Everything in the Universe* by Andrew Boyd. Copyright © 2002 by Andrew Boyd. Used by permission of W. W. Norton & Company, Inc.

Leo Buscaglia: Excerpt from *Love: What Life Is All About* by Leo Buscaglia. Copyright © 1972 by Leo F. Buscaglia, Inc. Reprinted by Permission of Random House, Inc.

Leonard Cohen: "Dance Me to the End of Love." Written by Leonard Cohen. © 1984 Sony/ATV Music Publishing LLC. All rights administered by Sony/ATV Music Publishing LLC, 8 Music Square West, Nashville, TN 37203. All rights reserved. Used by permission.

Billy Collins: "Litany" from *Nine Horses: Poems* by Billy Collins. Copyright © 2002 by Billy Collins. Reprinted by permission of Random House, Inc.

Roy Croft: "Love" by Roy Croft from *The Family Book of Best Loved Poems*, edited by David L. George. Copyright © 1952. Reprinted by permission of Hanover House, Doubleday.

E. E. Cummings: "somewhere i have never travelled,gladly beyond" by E. E. Cummings. Copyright © 1931, © 1959, 1991 by the Trustees for the E. E. Cummings Trust. Copyright © 1979 by George James Firmage, from *Complete Poems: 1904–1962* by E. E. Cummings, edited by George J. Firmage. Used by permission of Liveright Publishing Corporation.

Carol Ann Duffy: "Rings" by Carol Ann Duffy excerpted from "Poems for a wedding." *The Guardian*, April 22, 2011: 2. Print. Reprinted by permission of Guardian News and Media Limited.

Vidyapati: Hindu love poem from *In Praise of Krishna*, by E. C. Dimock and D. Levertov. Reprinted with the permission of The Asia Society.

William Carlos Williams: Excerpt from *Journey to Love* by William Carlos Williams, from *The Collected Poems: Volume I, 1909–1939*, copyright © 1938 by New Directions Publishing Corp. Reprinted by permission of New Directions Publishing Corp.

Here is a list of our additional sources for the book:

101 Classic Love Poems. Chicago: NTC/Contemporary Publishing Group, 1988.

Ackerman, Diane, and Jeanne Mackin, eds. *The Book of Love*. New York: W. W. Norton & Company, 1998.

Alighieri, Dante. *The Divine Comedy: Inferno, Purgatorio, Paradiso*. Translated by Allen Mandelbaum. New York: Alfred A. Knopf, 1995.

Brontë, Charlotte. *Jane Eyre*. New York: Penguin Classics, 1996.

Brontë, Emily. *Wuthering Heights*. New York: Penguin Classics, 1996.

Browning, Elizabeth Barrett. *Sonnets from the Portuguese*. New York: St. Martin's Press, 1986.

Byron, Lord George Gordon. *Lord Byron: The Major Works*. Edited by Jerome J. McGann. New York: Oxford University Press, Inc., 2008.

The Dhammapada. Translated by Balangoda Ananda Maitreya. Berkeley, CA: Parallax Press, 1995.

Dunbar, Paul Laurence. *The Collected Poetry of Paul Laurence Dunbar*. Edited by Joanne M. Braxton. Charlottesville, VA: University of Virginia Press, 1993.

Emerson, Ralph Waldo. *Ralph Waldo Emerson: Selected Poems and Translations*. Edited by Paul Kane and Harold Bloom. New York: Library of America, 1994.

Gardner, Helen Louise, ed. *The New Oxford Book of English Verse, 1250– 1950*. New York: Oxford University Press, Inc., 1972.

Martin, William. *The Couple's Tao Te Ching*. Boston: Da Capo Press, 1999.

Milton, John. *John Milton's Paradise Lost*. Edited by Harold Bloom. New York: Chelsea House Publishing, 2000.

Rossetti, Christina Georgina. *Christina Rossetti: Selected Poems*. New York: St. Martin's Press, 1995.

Shakespeare, William. *The Sonnets: William Shakespeare*. New York: Random House, 1997.

Sidney, Sir Philip. *Sir Philip Sidney: Selected Prose and Poetry*. Edited by Robert Kimbrough. Madison: The University of Wisconsin Press, 1994.

Simon, Raymond, ed. *Love Is Enough: Poems and Painting Celebrating Love*. Chicago: NTC/Contemporary Publishing Group, 2000.

University of Virginia, Electronic Text Center, Alderman Library, for Shoshone love poem (extext@Virginia.edu).

Whitman, Walt. *Leaves of Grass*. New York: Signet, 2000.

Woodring, Carl, and James Shapiro, eds. *The Columbia Anthology of British Poetry*. New York: Columbia University Press, 1995.

PHOTO CREDITS

10: Elizabeth Messina

13: Lindsay J. C. Lack

32: Bob and Dawn Davis Photography and Design

41: Elizabeth Messina

93: Desi Baytan Photography

98: Marie Labbancz Photography

103: Adi Nevo Photographs

113: Heather Saunders Photography

115: Paige Eden Photography

124: Clark+Walker Studio

127: Bob and Dawn Davis Photography and Design

129: B&G Photography

142: A Bryan Photo

152: Jane Bernard Photography

163: Jenna Walker Photographers

167: Maloman Photographers

INDEX